OREGON DISASTERS

DISASTERS SERIES

OREGON DISASTERS

TRUE STORIES OF

TRAGEDY AND SURVIVAL

Rachel Dresbeck

INSIDERS' GUIDE®

GUILFORD, CONNECTICUT

AN IMPRINT OF THE GLOBE PEQUOT PRESS

INSIDERS' GUIDE®

Text design by Pettistudio LLC, www.pettistudio.com
Map by M. A. Dubé © Morris Book Publishing, LLC

Library of Congress Cataloging-in-Publication Data
Dresbeck, Rachel.
Oregon disasters : true stories of tragedy and survival / Rachel Dresbeck. — 1st ed.
p. cm. — (Disasters series)
Includes bibliographical references.
ISBN-13: 978-0-7627-3993-6
ISBN-10: 0-7627-3993-2
1. Natural disasters—Oregon. 2. Disasters—Oregon. I. Title. II. Series.
GB5010.D74 2006
979.5—dc22
2006017419

Manufactured in the United States of America
First Edition/First Printing

For Tom

Contents

Acknowledgments

Studying disasters makes one grateful. I would therefore like to acknowledge the people who helped me write this book. First, thanks are due to my loyal brother Brian for his endurance and research assistance; to the folks at the Oregon History Center for theirs, as well; to my daughters Flannery and Cleo for being good sports; and to my Globe Pequot editors, Mike Urban, Amy Paradysz, and Dan Spinella, for their unfailing patience. Thanks are most especially due my husband, Tom, who knows disaster when he sees it and keeps me from becoming one.

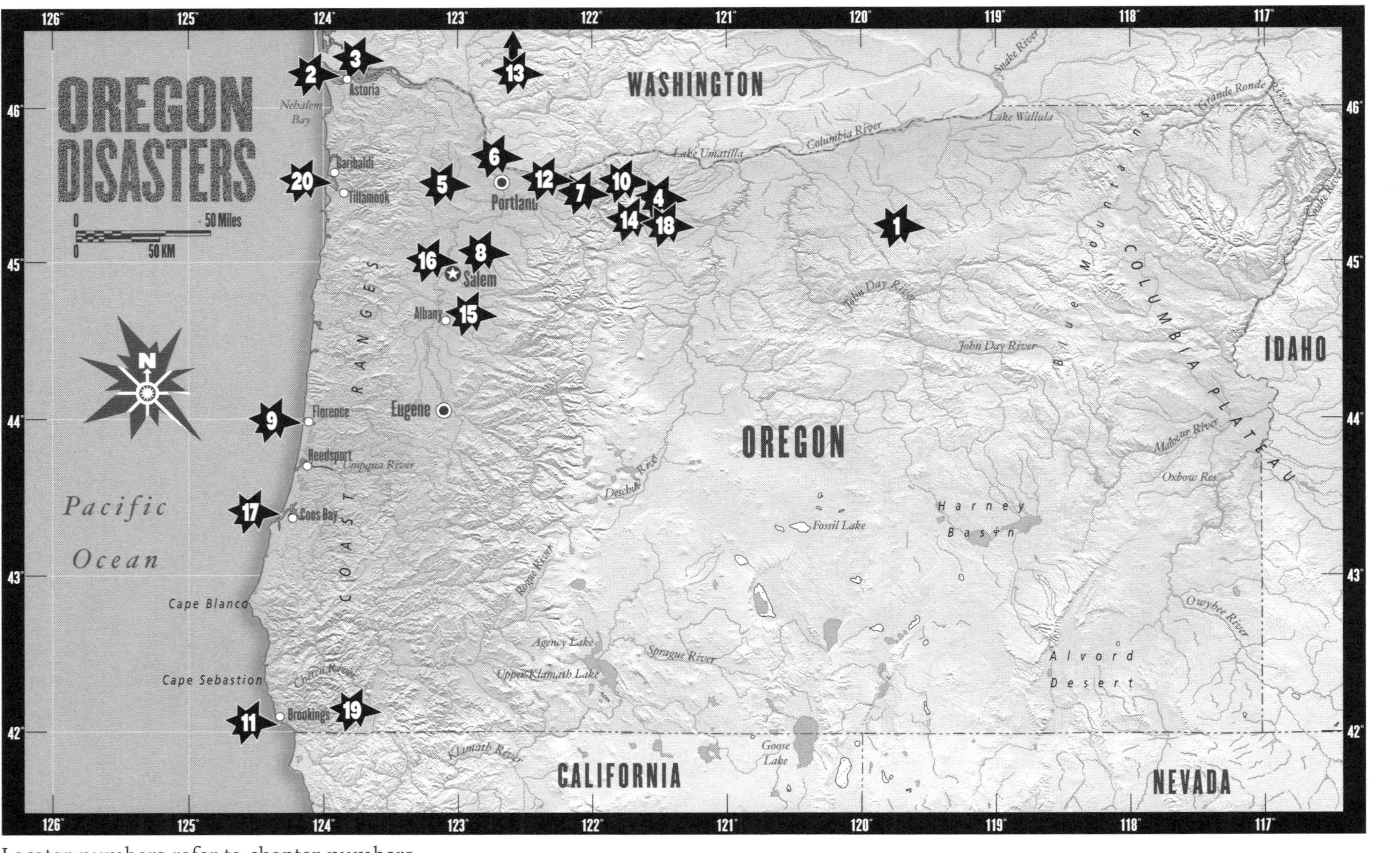

Locator numbers refer to chapter numbers.

Introduction

When it comes to disasters, Oregon is comparatively blessed and Oregonians lucky. We have yet to suffer a cataclysmic loss of life due to a massive earthquake, tsunami, or hurricane, even though we have experienced all of these. Our large fires happen in remote forests, and the ships that wreck off the Oregon coast don't hold that many people. When airliners crash, people walk away from the accident—at least so far. On the whole, our number has not yet come up.

At the individual level, however, we see plenty of disaster, and how we face disasters as individuals is an important theme of this book. *Oregon Disasters* tells the tale of twenty such incidents. The stories in this book were chosen for their scale and scope—not necessarily for how many people died, but whether the event had a deep or long-lasting influence, whether it wrought changes to landscapes, lives, practices, or policies. The largest loss of life came in 1903, as described in this book's first chapter, when a flash flood engulfed the town of Heppner, killing nearly 300 people. Since then, our disasters have involved fewer fatalities.

An important criterion was that the events were not precipitated by malice. Thus, I left out one notable incident: the first act of bioterrorism in the United States, when a religious cult poisoned a salad bar in a central Oregon town with salmonella bacteria, hoping to change the outcome of an election. Despite that omission we still had plenty of other tales. Readers familiar with Oregon's reputation for rain will not be surprised to learn that rain was part of many of the disasters—floods, hurricanes, and shipwrecks. But a lack of rain also plays a role in several stories: two major forest fires (in 1933 and 2002) and the incineration of the town of Astoria in 1922. The coastal waters off Oregon are another source of mishap and tragedy, so I included several incidents involving shipwrecks off the coast.

Many of our disasters involve another noted feature of Oregon: our beloved mountains and the adventures they inspire. The sport of mountain climbing was popularized in Oregon, and especially on Mount Hood, and many climbers have been lost on its slopes. I tell some of their stories here. I also included the eruption of Mount St. Helens, even though it is in Washington, because Mount St. Helens is a dominant feature of the landscape in Portland. It is viewed daily by more Oregonians than Washingtonians. Finally, I also included some stories that are obscure even to Oregonians but that deserve attention—such as the loss of thirteen people off the coast of Brookings in August 1972.

Rescues are important, also. The philosopher Seneca noted that the point of life is not to live long but to live nobly. Many of the heroic figures in this book did both—notably, Bruce Kelly and Les Matlock, two men who warned their neighbors that a great flash flood was headed their way. Also included is an unlikely hero, a convict on United Flight 173, who assisted his fellow passengers off the destroyed airliner and then disappeared into the night.

How an individual will respond to events is perhaps the great puzzle of existence, a puzzle that is more complex the deeper one gets into it. For example, while many, and perhaps even most, of these stories involve the weather in some way—forest fires, shipwrecks, floods, hurricanes, blizzards—the weather is often the proximate cause. The direct cause of a disaster may be the choices made by individuals. It may be a failure to make the right decision: Should I cross the bar? Should I go up the mountain? Should we haul that last log out of the underbrush? Should we try burning off the excess oil? In hindsight, the answer often is: probably not.

Such judgments are too easy to make in hindsight. No one sets out to make the wrong decision, after all. Many disasters are brought about by conscientious persons trying to make the right decision. The crash of United Flight 173, the botched salvage operations of the *Mimi* and the *New Carissa,* and the wreck of the *Taki-Tooo* are all examples of this phenomenon.

When contemplating disaster, it is tempting to mull over platitudes and draw lessons. And, of course, it is good to feel that suffering has not been in vain, and that we can learn from events. Indeed, we have learned a great deal about volcanoes and forest fires, floods and tsunamis. We have learned how to climb mountains more safely and to be cautious conducting agricultural burns. Yet, even in Oregon, tragedy may bring no lesson and nothing to say. Some things must be regarded in silence.

CHAPTER 1

DEATH AND DESTRUCTION IN ITS WAKE

The Heppner Flood

1903

Heppner is a quiet town in eastern Oregon. Most Oregonians have never been to Heppner unless they happened to be driving through it on the way somewhere else, and many have never even heard of the place. But Heppner was the scene of the worst natural disaster ever to befall Oregon: On June 14, 1903, a flash flood ripped through the town, killing nearly one-fourth of its population in a matter of moments.

Nestled into the grassy hills just west of the Blue Mountains, nearly 200 miles east of Portland, Heppner lies along a confluence of creeks in Morrow County, an oasis in a golden prairie. The surrounding hills offer prime land for rich grazing and wheat farming. This is not the Oregon of lush forests and pristine beaches. It is hot and dry and treeless. At Heppner, however, four creeks merge—Hinton, Shobe, Balm Fork, and Willow—providing the town with the water it needs for respite and survival.

In 1903 Heppner was a flourishing farming town of nearly 1,400 people. It had grown beyond its pioneer beginnings and become an established community; it had been designated the county seat, and just the year before, it had constructed a handsome stone courthouse. Heppner was a hub of agricultural activity, sending out wool, cattle, and wheat to other parts of Oregon and beyond. Not only had Heppner weathered the economic depression of the 1890s, which devastated much of the United States, but it had actually prospered, more than doubling its population between 1890 and 1903. For a remote farming town, Heppner was sophisticated. Residents could boast that their town had two hotels—the Heppner Hotel and the beautiful brick Palace Hotel—as well as two banks, a number of saloons, numerous churches, and a large steam laundry. The residents lived on shady poplar-lined streets in pretty, two-story clapboard houses with late-Victorian cupolas, scrolls, and curlicues. Most of the houses lay along Willow Creek for a stretch of 2 miles. Thus, Heppner was the very picture of frontier success, emblematic of the Oregon dream that had lured so many from the Midwest and beyond. Indeed, Heppner even had numerous residents who had originally settled in western Oregon but who returned east, yearning for the beautiful expanse of open prairie and fleeing, perhaps, the sodden rains of the west.

June 14, 1903, dawned fair and bright, but as the day wore on, heavy, black clouds gathered, and by 4:30 P.M., Heppner was enduring a severe summer rainstorm. It was good news, for the spring of 1903 was unusually dry and hot, jeopardizing the crops and the livelihood of the entire town. Three days before, on June 11, another savage thunderstorm had dropped several inches of rain on the area and caused some minor flooding, so this second storm perhaps signaled the end of the drought. People moved inside to watch it, and, as the *Heppner Gazette* later noted, since the amount of rainfall was not alarming, the residents of Heppner were happy about the weather, for "a good soaking rain was needed to help out the crops." But as 5:00 approached, the people of Heppner stopped preparing for Sunday evening services at the church, stopped serving tea to their visitors, put down their newspapers and sewing, and just watched the storm as it gathered in intensity. It began to hail, and fierce winds, thunder, and lightning shook the town in a furious squall that made it impossible for the residents to hear one another speak.

Eight miles up the creek, the storm was even fiercer. Balm Fork, which trickles into Willow Creek, was deluged with rain and hail, overflowing its banks as it had three days before. But this time, it was joined by similar torrents from all the other feeders into Willow Creek, setting in motion a wave that began to collect silt, branches, trees, and rocks. As the waters from the overfilled creeks surged toward Heppner, they collected more from the farms that the creeks ran beside; they collected tree branches and logs and rubbish, and a silty, debris-filled wall of water hurtled toward the town.

At the southern edge of the town was the steam laundry, a large wooden building that was built across Willow Creek to take advantage of its flow. Now, as the waters built up in the raging creek, the laundry served as dam. But it could not withstand the pressure. The water burst through the building, and the laundry owners and their employees were the first to drown in the great flood of 1903.

Meanwhile, some residents noticed that the creeks were overflowing and grew concerned. About thirty people sought higher ground on a small hill behind one of the banks. From there, they could see Willow, Hinton, and Balm Fork Creeks swelling. They had to shout to one another to be heard, so great

The June 1903 flood struck Heppner by surprise, killing one-quarter of the town's population. PHOTO COURTESY NATIONAL WEATHER SERVICE PORTLAND

was the volume of the thunder, hail, and rain. Some of them were about to return to lower ground when suddenly a tremendous rush of water blew through Balm Fork, severing Willow Creek.

But at 5 P.M., when that 40-foot wall of water hit the town of Heppner, most failed to hear it coming. Many downtown residents only realized that something was wrong when their houses began to move. As people became aware of just what was bearing down upon them, they retreated to the hillsides, out of the reach of the waters, where they helplessly watched their town—their families, friends, neighbors, their animals and houses and buildings—swept away in minutes. They watched as many perished. They watched as poplar trees 2 feet in diameter snapped like breadsticks. They watched as large buildings floated away, dragged by the water off their foundations, then crashed into other structures, shattering them in the process and adding to the swell of debris.

"The first warning that the people in the business portion had was when the large two-story residence building of T. W. Ayers left its foundation and swung around into May Street and crashed into and lodged on some wooden buildings just back of the Palace Hotel," reported the *Heppner Gazette*. Mr. Ayers was attending to business at the powerhouse. His family ran upstairs as their house began to move, safely escaping when the building finally came to rest.

Considering the volume of water and its speed, it was remarkable that anyone survived the flood. Many escaped by running to higher ground, but among those who were caught up in the deluge, it was a matter of whether they could hold onto some floating thing long enough to be swept onto dry land. Those who attempted to swim the flood perished. A number of people managed to survive by clinging to the wreckage of their buildings. Dan Salter watched as his wife and six of his children drowned, but he and his remaining son were able to grab a dry goods box floating by and use it to ride to shore. Another man, Phil Cohn, had been sleeping and awoke to find his house being smashed to pieces all around him in a torrent of water. But he managed to salvage a board, hanging onto it as the water pulled him under several times, until it spit him out into a nearby alfalfa field. Likewise, Julius Keithley was saved, ironically, by the destruction of his own home. Keithley was determined to stay with his house, and stay with it he did, until nothing but the roof remained. This he used as a raft, riding it for nearly

2 miles, and along the way pulling another survivor, William Ayers, to safety.

Other witnesses describe equally improbable escapes. The Conser family was entertaining visitors when the flood struck, and their visitors—Dr. McSwords, J. L. Ayers, and a servant—ran out of the house only to be caught up in the flood. All three drowned. Mr. and Mrs. Conser instead hastened upstairs, just in time to see the lower half of their building wash away, allowing the top story to sink and settle—and they along with it. Soon the Consers were up to their necks in water, but as their house began to move, it came to rest against another building, stabilizing it long enough for the Consers to get to a window, where they were pulled out of the flood by rescuers. The Minor family also ran upstairs when the water hit and reported watching as the first story of their building disintegrated, the wreckage bobbing like twigs in the water. They too were at the verge of drowning, when the upper part of their house lodged against a church, and they escaped through a window.

One young mother, Cora Phelps, wrote a long letter to a friend, detailing her experience of watching the storm while she nursed her baby. She had been home on a Sunday afternoon with her husband Bert and another couple. They watched as the two creeks near the house, Hinton and Willow, began to fill rapidly and then spill over their banks. Cora watched Bert pull on his coat and boots—and then hurry back inside. He had seen the bridges ripped away by the waters. And just as he made it in the door, Cora wrote, the flood came rushing down their street, tearing houses off their foundations.

> It almost makes me sick when I think about it, for if he had not gotten in just the minute he did, I feel that he would

> have been swept away. When we met him downstairs, the water and mud rushed into our house about two feet deep and I will never forget how cold it was. Bert said give me the baby for he knew that she was the smallest and most helpless and, of course, [our daughter] Margaret couldn't walk through it so I picked her up and Bert told us to all go upstairs. I will never forget how thoughtful and brave he was, and he had so much hope. I never had the least ray of hope, I thought the world was coming to an end.

An hour after the flood began, it was over. But hundreds had vanished and where there once was a prosperous little town laid catastrophe. More than 140 buildings in the small town were destroyed; the residential area was obliterated and only three buildings remained in the business district. Heppner was also cut off from the world when it badly needed help—the roads were ruined, the rail line washed away, and the telegraph and telephone wires wiped out.

Meanwhile, two residents began to worry about the towns downstream of the flood. Les Matlock and Bruce Kelly were range riders and lifelong friends who knew the land well. Both were standing on a hill at the edge of town, where they had a clear view of the flooding. They could see that the next towns along Willow Creek—Lexington and Ione—would be engulfed by the rushing waters.

Kelly told Matlock that the flood was bound to drown everyone living on the creek below Heppner. Matlock replied that if they had horses, perhaps the two of them could warn those in the path of the flood. So Kelly went off to see if the stable where they kept their horses still stood, while Matlock went to a hardware store that was still standing to get some wire cutters—

they would be needed to cut fences if the two were going to ride over the range. Since it was Sunday, the store was closed and boarded up, and he had to kick in the door; then he had trouble finding wire cutters in the pitch-black store. But a few moments later, he emerged with some wooden-handled pruning shears as Bruce Kelly was returning from the stable with the horses—not their horses, but the ones he could find. They rode off over the range, racing the flood down the valley.

The two men could not see much, for by now it was nightfall. But the storm was still raging and lighting would brighten the sky for a moment. Matlock and Kelly could not take the road, which followed the creek and would have proven deadly. They had to ride through the backcountry, where their progress was slowed by rocks, hills, and the countless barbed-wire fences that had to be individually cut, fences that carried electrical charges from the storm. At the very first fence, as if to warn the two riders of the danger, they found a dead horse—had it been struck by lightning? Had it electrocuted itself on the fence? It wasn't clear, but the horse served them notice. Kelly said to Matlock that he would be killed if he cut the wires. But Matlock replied that he was pretty sure all of his relatives and most of his friends were drowned, and he didn't really care what happened to him, so he may as well cut the wire.

This was the first of many charged fences that they had to manage, but these were not the only dangers. The ride was hard on the horses and their riders. Matlock's horse, which was an old workhorse unnerved by the storm, stepped into a badger hole and threw him off. It was frustratingly slow going. They could not hear one another in the noise of the storm, and they couldn't see anything in its terrible blackness.

Matlock and Kelly made it to the first town, Lexington, just after the flood had reached it. It was too late to save Lexington, but they thought they could make it to Ione, 9 miles away. They stopped for a moment to check on a farmer they knew, Andrew Rainey, and he gave Matlock a better horse. Then they were off, flying over the hills, hoping to beat the flood.

And by driving their horses hard, they succeeded. They called to the farmhouses that they passed, urging people to head for higher ground. They reached Ione about an hour before the flood, split up, and sounded the alarm all through the town.

Contemporary accounts note that the "astonished" residents of the little town were just getting ready for evening church services when the riders appeared bearing the grim news. The townsfolk made a mad scramble up surrounding hillsides, then watched as the waters rushed through their town, wreaking destruction. Ione suffered much damage and few buildings were left, yet thanks to Matlock and Kelly, not a single person died.

Back in Heppner, heartbroken people had to start cleaning up the slime and debris. Seventy million pounds of water, silt, and wreckage had flowed through the town, destroying everything in its path. One building left standing was the Palace Hotel, a well-built structure that had helped to divert and slow the waters headed toward the central business district of town. The Palace Hotel organized a soup kitchen to feed the survivors, and the residents began the search for the missing. By the next morning, local officials had begun to worry about the threat to public health presented by the dead. Because the weather was so hot that year, it was imperative that bodies were recovered quickly. One of the other remaining buildings, a fine stone structure called the Roberts Building, became a makeshift morgue, where bodies were cleaned before making their final journey to Heppner Cemetery, sometimes before they were even identified.

Word of Heppner's misfortune soon reached the rest of Oregon and eastern Washington. One boy of fifteen, Guy Boyer, had ridden northeast to the small town of Echo, a distance of nearly 50 miles, right after the flood. At Echo, he was able to take a train to Pendleton and alert the world of Heppner's plight. A week after the disaster, money began to arrive to assist the residents in their clean-up efforts and help restore order to the town. Small towns across the region had collected money for their upcoming Fourth of July celebrations, and many of these towns donated those funds to the citizens of Heppner. Even children helped—some young girls in Colfax, Washington, about 100 miles to the north, raised money from selling cakes and flowers and sent it to Heppner. Altogether, more than $1 million in relief money (calculated in today's figures) was raised.

While a number of the flood's survivors moved away, more stayed, and they rebuilt the town. But it took nearly a century for Heppner's population to rebuild itself. Today, for the 1,400 residents, there are few traces of the Heppner Flood—unless you know where to look. In Heppner Cemetery a memorial stone and 247 headstones—the official death count—bear witness to the date of June 14, 1903. No one can really be sure if all the dead were accounted for, however, and many believed that some bodies were never recovered, that perhaps some were swept nearly 50 miles to the Columbia River, with no one to testify to their fate. Much of the town's architecture dates from 1903, providing unspoken reminders of the year of the flood. The street that runs in front of the Morrow County Courthouse is called Matlock Street, in honor of the town's hero. In 2003 the town of Heppner renamed the street that runs in front of the cemetery "Bruce Kelly Drive." Along the creek traces of the flood are even more elusive. Willow Creek flooded twice more, in 1941 and in 1978, but today it is controlled by a dam. Local residents swim in the reservoir that the dam has created, and a country club lies farther downstream. Heppner has recovered.

Bruce Kelly died in 1943 of natural causes, well into his seventies. Leslie Matlock died at age eighty-four in 1958. Both men were honored throughout their lives, especially Matlock. By all accounts he was a thoughtful, wise, and charming man who dismissed any characterization of himself as a hero. He said anyone would have done what he did under the circumstances. Before he died, he told a friend that he remembered the flood of 1903 clearly. He remembered the great walls of water that thundered down Willow Creek. He remembered the mighty surge of water that rushed down Balm Fork. And he remembered when the two creeks became one. "What a terrible sight that was," he said. "Even now I sometimes wake up in the night after dreaming I was drowning. Now I often think of the terrible days that followed."

CHAPTER 2

DEAD MAN'S HOTEL

The Wreck of the *Mimi*

1913

Captain Westphal leveled a pistol at his crew. "I will shoot the first man who leaves this ship," he said. The captain was trying to keep any more sailors from deserting the *Mimi,* a German square-rigger sailing ship with masts reaching 200 feet. It had benignly run aground several months before, and now they were trying to refloat the ship.

Sailors can be superstitious, though, and that morning, Saturday, April 5, 1913, the *Mimi*'s second-in-command had awoken from terrifying dreams. The ship had become a dead man's hotel, he dreamed. He saw the *Mimi* resting on the ocean floor. All but the captain and two men were there. Seaweed wreathed their heads, and their faces were enshrouded in fog. This dream unnerved the officer, Frederick Flagg, completely. He related his dream to the two other mates. They felt something was about to go very wrong, a feeling so powerful that it overrode their innate sense of duty to Captain Westphal. This was serious business. German officers never deserted their ships. Nevertheless, the three officers headed for shore, slipping down the cables that held the *Mimi* fast.

Theirs was an easy journey, for the *Mimi* had run aground 800 feet out on the north spit of Nehalem Bay, Oregon, within sight of the shore. At ebb tide the ship was partly out of water, and it was an easy walk to dry land. On February 13, the crew of the *Mimi* had become lost in the fog and mistook the Nehalem jetty for a sign that they had reached their destination, the Columbia River. Sailing just north of the jetty, the ship ran into a sandbar and found itself stuck. The *Mimi* was not much damaged and remained upright, though held fast in the sand.

A few miles to the north, at the Coast Guard's Garibaldi Life Saving Station, Capt. Robert Farley heard about the ship, and he took his surfboat and crew north to Nehalem to see what kind of help he might offer. Captain Farley was a talented and doughty sailor who had saved the lives of many. From spending much of his time rescuing sailors, he had some insight into the things that made ships run aground, tip over, and sink. In this case, though, Captain Farley's efforts were not needed. The grounded ship itself was the only thing that required rescuing.

When a ship runs aground, the first task is to rescue the crew, and the second is to see if the ship is salvageable. There was every reason to salvage the *Mimi*. It had sustained no major damage, and it was in a good position to be refloated. It stood in about 7 feet of water, resting up against the sandbank. Leading marine salvage experts were called in, and they all agreed it would be worth the money to salvage the ship. The Fisher Salvage Company from Brighton—the town that was due east of the ship—was hired to dig the *Mimi* out of the sand and send her back to sea.

The residents of the area took great interest in the planned salvage, scheduled for Sunday, April 6. Everyone was suddenly an expert on salvaging ships, and there was much public com-

A postcard of the Mimi *on Neah-Kah-Nie Beach, February 13, 1913.*
FROM THE COLLECTION OF ROXANN GESS SMITH

ment and analysis and advice for Capt. Charles Fisher, president of the salvage company and leader of the salvage operation. He and his men worked with the crew of the *Mimi,* who were mostly from Germany and were being hosted by local German immigrant families. Together, they were confident that the *Mimi* would soon be afloat.

The salvage engineers chose April 6 in order to take advantage of an extreme flood tide. The plan was to place two four-ton anchors offshore and then link the anchors to two barges. The barges would draw two massive cables from the *Mimi*. Engines on the barges and on the *Mimi* were prepared for the task, fitted with giant winches to feed and take up the cable from the *Mimi* as the ship made her way back to sea. To make the ship easier to float and maneuver, the salvage engineers took out about one-third of the ballast, 1,300 tons. This decision, however, was controversial. It generated much discussion among observing amateurs and professionals alike—including Captain Farley—who were concerned about what would happen when the *Mimi* reached the breakers. The ship was tall and large; its masts stretched 200 feet. It needed its ballast to keep it under control. But Fisher disagreed.

The day of salvage became a sort of local holiday, and everything from canneries to sawmills shut down in preparation for it. The *Mimi's* fourteen sailors and the twelve salvage crew expected success. Captains Fisher and Crowe of the salvage company expected it. The community—including the townsfolk, the experts, and the newspapers—expected success. There was no reason not to expect it. The *Mimi* was close to shore and everyone involved was a consummate professional.

As April 5 dawned, however, the signs grew less auspicious. First, Frederick Flagg had his dream and abandoned ship with two other needed hands. Saturday's work went well otherwise, but Robert Farley remained troubled about the removal of the ballast. He visited Captain Westphal on the *Mimi* to express his concern that once the ship hit the breakers, it would capsize. The chief engineer of the salvage crew, who perhaps was beginning to tire of all the well-meaning advice, overheard this conversation. He did not appreciate having his judgment second-guessed. He took Westphal aside and they spoke for a few minutes. "When we need you, sir, we'll let you know," Westphal told Farley. But Farley worried that by the time Westphal got around to letting him know, it would be too late.

Sunday arrived, and the much-anticipated salvage event began at first light.

Meanwhile, at Captain Farley's lifesaving station, word arrived that a storm was on its way. Farley sent up the hurricane flags and put his crew on constant watch. He also called the headquarters of the salvage company. He told them about the storm—and that if they proceeded with the salvage on that day, they would be imperiling the crew of the *Mimi* and their own salvage engineers. "And probably the lives of my men," he added. Captain Fisher had heard quite enough from Farley. He told Farley what he could do with his storm warnings and other concerns and hung up the telephone. Farley was furious.

On the *Mimi* the salvage work continued apace, in spite of the strong winds and violent surf. The tide was in. The moment had arrived. The crew fired up the engines on the barges and the engine on the *Mimi* and released the shore cables. The offshore cables tightened against the anchors, and the ship began to slowly advance. On shore, in spite of the rain, a large crowd was gathering to watch.

In the beginning progress was excellent, and the *Mimi* crept along just as she was supposed to. But the wind was beginning to pick up speed. When the *Mimi* reached deeper water, she began to roll and sway. The crowd on the beach could see what was coming, and on the *Mimi,* Captain Westphal decided to halt operations—he could see that the position of the ship was too treacherous. But just as he approached the sailors manning the engines, the *Mimi* began to move crazily from side to side. Then it suddenly rolled completely over.

Captain Westphal later recalled:

> As I was walking forward to tell the donkey engine not to pull the *Mimi* further seaward but to anchor her where she was, a sudden lurch took the vessel and I was pinned to the forward deckhouse by a fallen top spar. This lurch immediately preceded the capsizing of the *Mimi.* I distinctly remember

The Mimi *ran aground 800 feet out on Newhalem Spit, within sight of shore, making the ship's rescue effort quite the spectacle.*
PHOTO COURTESY TILLAMOOK COUNTY PIONEER MUSEUM

> hearing Capt. Crowe speaking, but when we reached there, no one was to be seen. Nor were there any signs of life on the forward part of the ship at all. The donkey engine, mounted there, had slid into the sea.

Robert Farley had predicted just this scenario. He weighed his options. He could see the exposed deck of the *Mimi* and the hatches open to the sea. Everything he had feared had come to pass, and now he had to decide whether to risk the lives of his own men to save those aboard the *Mimi*. Adding to his pressures was the very public scrutiny he knew he would receive no matter what his decision—after all, the whole town had gathered on the beach to watch the salvage, and of course the newspapers were there to report on the event of the season.

He decided to launch the lifesaving boat.

Conditions were grim. The sea raged, the rains were drenching, and the winds were vicious. Even before they left the beach, the lifesaving crew was wet and shivering. It took a long time to reach the *Mimi*. It was on its starboard side, mired in the masts, sails, and rigging that had come down with the ship. Farley and his men struggled to get close, blocked by the impassable gyre of debris. The lifesaving crew made it to within 50 yards, but they nearly capsized several times as they attempted to pass through the wreckage. The lifesaving crew searched for survivors but saw no sign of life. The bowman spotted the body of one of the wrecking crew floating face down in the water. They drew him in, but saw no one else, living or dead. Farley thought perhaps everyone had drowned. But there was no way to find out: They could neither board the *Mimi* nor rig a line from shore, given the chaos of the stormy sea. They had little choice but to turn around.

During this very time Captain Westphal lay trapped by the forward yard, which had fallen when the *Mimi* first capsized. A couple of the young sailors saved the captain's life by freeing him, and together they searched the ship for survivors. They found Captain Fisher of the salvage crew and another sailor, from the *Mimi,* clinging to the lifeboat that had been stowed on the afterdeck. The sailor, Tom Koen, was almost submerged in the freezing waters, calling for help. Captain Westphal, Captain Fisher, and the other sailors passed a line under him and raised him about two feet, but Koen was a heavy man and they couldn't raise him any higher. Koen himself then, through an extreme effort of will, hoisted himself out of the water by swinging his legs over a spar attached to the bulwark. This effort, however, seemed to drain the remaining life from him, and Westphal reported that two minutes after he regained the ship, he died peacefully.

Captain Westphal no longer had his pistol, but he spent two hours attempting to convince his remaining men not to abandon ship, telling them that they would be safer on the ship than trying to swim to shore in such dangerous seas, no matter how close to shore they were; that they were protected by the 7-foot board that ran around the entire ship; and that eventually they would be rescued. Nevertheless, his men began to leap overboard, wagering that they could make it. One by one, they perished. One sailor had already thrown himself into the sea after the first lurch, even before the *Mimi* capsized, and he was lost. Others were crushed by the debris or simply drowned. Or they died of exposure, like Tom Koen.

What little hope the remaining sailors may have had seemed to evaporate with the return to shore of the lifesaving crew. No one was happy with Captain Farley and his men, especially after they reached the shore and gently removed the body of the dead sailor. The angry crowd, not having a thorough perspective of the great danger the lifesaving crew endured, urged them to go back out. They could see waves of 30 feet laying siege to the *Mimi,* often blocking her from sight.

Those aboard the *Mimi* vainly called to shore for three hours. Finally, they attempted to attract attention by climbing up into the part of the ship that was not submerged—a dangerous undertaking under those conditions. Meanwhile, on shore the three mates who had deserted the *Mimi* were even more anxious for their comrades. All at once, a buzz erupted from the crowd on the shore: The *Mimi* had made contact—white flags waved through an open porthole.

Farley thought about his men. His frozen crew were finally warming themselves at a fire that some fishermen had built for them. The tide was reaching its low point, which made the *Mimi* more accessible but increased the violence of the surf. Yet if there were signs of life on the *Mimi,* they had to try to help the stranded sailors. Farley ordered his men to sea once more. It was 4:30 and it was getting dark. Again, the lifesaving boat nearly capsized in the breakers. They could not maneuver their boat, and the great current sent them past the *Mimi*. Time after time, they attempted to reach the wreck, but they could not fight the giant swells. They had to accept defeat and return to shore, exhausted and frozen. Once there, they repeatedly attempted to reach the ship with a cable gun, fighting wind so strong that it was impossible to get the line to the target.

The rage of the crowd was palpable. The surfmen were accused of cowardice—and drunkenness, for some witnesses saw them stumbling as the cold and wet sailors worked their way toward the fire at the beach. Some of the *Mimi*'s regular crew, including the three who had abandoned the ship, asked Farley if they could take out the surfboat themselves. Farley angered the crowd further by saying no—it was too risky.

Adding to the controversy were reporters from the local papers, who smelled a good story. Indeed, by the next day one paper would give a sympathetic account of the ordeal, while the other would accuse Farley of criminal behavior. Yet the crew had been attempting to rescue sailors who by all common sense should not have been in danger. If Captain Farley had been heeded in the first place, the *Mimi*'s sailors would be alive, and the lifesaving crew would not be frozen, thirsty, hungry, and exhausted, having risked their lives all day and into the night to rescue them.

The lifesaving crew tried once again to reach the *Mimi* before dark, with no success. The sailors on the *Mimi* witnessed these attempts. Captain Westphal explained their feelings:

> With the coming of darkness we gave ourselves up for goners, as we knew the tide was higher than that of the night before—and that almost covered the boat. . . . The most sickening feeling anyone could have was experienced when the last attempt at rescue failed Sunday night. It looked as though our lives were to sink out with the dying sun.

Farley was wretched. What could be worse than seeing this ship founder so close to shore? While the crowd on shore was angry at the surfmen, it was an understandable response to their own feelings of helplessness and horror. Farley knew he had done the right thing not to further endanger the lives of his men. Yet was there a chance—any chance—that he had missed an opportunity to save those aboard the *Mimi?* Was there something else he could have done? He was an experienced captain and had been involved in many rescues, but he was not about to risk more lives.

That night was a long, dark one for those on the *Mimi*. Westphal, Fisher, and the two other surviving sailors attempted to keep up their spirits, recounting all the tales they'd heard of wrecks even worse than this one that had come out all right in the end. "We prayed and hoped and clung," said Westphal, "paralyzed from the cold, sickened by exposure, and faint from hunger and thirst. The smell of the sea was horrible."

At dawn on Monday the seas were finally calm. On board the *Mimi* the few survivors watched hopefully as Captain Farley and his men set out once again. Using all their expertise, the crew maneuvered the rescue boat into a 10-foot-wide space underneath the bulwarks of the *Mimi,* between the ship and one of its spars that was lodged in the sand underneath the ship. Though the water was calmer, the ship remained in the treacherous breaker zone, so the lifesaving crew had to keep its boat from smashing against the *Mimi.* At last, though, they were able to reach the ship and search for anyone who might still be alive.

Farley found Captain Westphal, who told him three others were still alive. Westphal handed an unconscious young sailor, who had spent the last two days in freezing waters, into the lifeboat. Next came the cabin boy, who was able to get into the boat on his own. Then Captain Westphal and Captain Fisher, president of the salvage company, were hustled into the rescue boat and returned to shore.

Back on shore, Westphal related his wretched tale and told Farley that at least two of the *Mimi* crew had died that first night, and that these two were lashed to spars under the bulwarks. He did not know what exactly had happened to the rest of his men or Captain Fisher's. Captain Farley, in turn related the attempts at rescue, and Westphal agreed that Farley had done everything in his power. The unconscious sailor was given hot water and mustard treatments until he revived, and the other survivors were wrapped in blankets and given hot whiskey. During these ministrations one of the three mates who had jumped ship intruded, upset and angry, clamoring for the rescue boat to return to the ship to retrieve the corpses of his comrades. Farley refused. He would not risk the life and health of his men one more time. He promised the mate that he would return at low tide, after all had rested, and he did.

Captain Fisher was also miserable. Of his experience, he said:

> My whole life put together did not seem as long as the hours between Sunday and daybreak this morning. It seemed years. All we could do was wait. Often during the long hours I thought I would give up my hold and fall into the water to join the others we knew had gone before us. Several times I lost heart but something seemed to cause me to cling. I was frozen with the cold of the water, was sickened by the cries of the people about us, and was faint from hunger and thirst. I cannot see how I held on as long as I did.

The aftermath of the rescue was difficult. Whenever tragedy strikes, we look to blame someone—if not the gods, then the authorities. But who should be blamed? Captain Westphal was a candidate—perhaps he should have let his men desert the ship after all. But Fritz Ludwig, the sailor who had been unconscious, stated that the sailors felt no ill will toward Westphal, even though he had threatened them. "It was his duty to prevent desertion," he said, and when they found the captain trapped by the fallen spar, he observed, "It was our duty to help him." Suspicion especially fell on Captain Farley. Even before the rescue boat had reached the shore with the survivors, one of the Tillamook papers accused Farley of incompetence, claiming that he and his men were cowards and drunks. When the federal investigators arrived a few weeks later, as they always must after a shipwreck, they interviewed many witnesses to see if these charges were warranted. The local fishermen, however, came to the defense of the rescuers—they knew well what Farley and his crew had been up against, and every one of them testified in Farley's favor. The investigators' report filed in Washington, D.C., pointedly observed that there no shred of evidence that Farley or his men were drunk, and that in fact most of the blame lay with the head of the wrecking firm, Captain Fisher. He ought to have been more cognizant of his own role in the disaster, the report opined, for "there had been criminal carelessness on his own part or the bark would not have capsized. Had Farley listened to the clamor of the crowd and tried to put out through the wreckage, another tragedy would have occurred."

Twenty-one sailors were aboard the *Mimi* that day, and seventeen of them died. Other shipwrecks off the treacherous Oregon coast have cost more lives, but few wrecks have been as wasteful as the loss of the *Mimi*.

CHAPTER 3

PORT TOWN IN FLAMES

The Astoria Fire

1922

The history of Astoria, Oregon, like the history of everywhere, begins with the shape of the land. Astoria is bordered to the north and west by water, for it lies at the mouth of the Columbia River, where the river meets the Pacific Ocean. In this mild, damp climate, the first Eastern settlers found massive Douglas fir trees to use for fuel, transportation, and building materials.

Astoria is the oldest city in Oregon—and not only the oldest in Oregon, but also one of the oldest in the American West. Few cities in Oregon have as colorful a history. It was founded on April 12, 1811, by some fur traders working for John Jacob Astor, of the great New York merchant family. Astor hoped to establish a fur trading post that could disrupt the monopoly the British had on that line of business. This first outpost was near the site where Meriwether Lewis and William Clark had spent a soggy and miserable winter five years before.

Astor's men duly created a successful trading post that was productive for about a year. Then the War of 1812 began, and the Oregon territory, including Astoria, remained in dispute for the next thirty years. For most of that time, the British retained control over the territory. Of course it depends on what a person means by "control," since whatever politicians in Washington, D.C., and London thought, the land was really "controlled" by the Chinook, Clatsop, and other tribes who had lived along the Columbia for eons.

Regardless of who was in charge, early settlements were small. But then, in 1846, Astoria was refounded by the United States. The Chinook and Clatsop gradually were crowded out by settlers from the East. Within a few years the town had become a comparatively bustling frontier metropolis. Its site had many advantages—it is a river port, overlooking a beautiful bay, and just beyond that, the Pacific Ocean. It is nestled into sloping, wooded hills. Even now, it is an important shipping harbor, though tourism has gradually taken the place of much of the salmon fishing, logging, and other industries, as it has everywhere else in Oregon.

But Astoria doesn't look like a picturesque frontier town built in the era of giant fir trees. If you visit downtown Astoria today, it looks much more like the location of Steven Spielberg's film *The Goonies*—which it was—than the oldest city in Oregon. While beautiful Victorian houses line the hillsides, most of downtown Astoria's architecture is unremarkable mid-twentieth-century storefront. And this is the legacy of fire. For on a cold, dry night in December 1922, a terrible fire destroyed 28 blocks of downtown Astoria.

Fire had come to Astoria several times before that night, as it did to most pioneer towns. A fire in 1883 had begun in a sawmill; the blaze devoured the waterfront in the course of several hours. Wharves and warehouses were destroyed, as were several blocks of houses and a number of saloons. Well-meaning citizens tried to save the liquor from the fire, rolling barrels of whiskey to safety, but as they ran back and forth from saloon to safety, Astoria's less-ambitious citizens began opening the barrels and consuming the liquor.

This activity was not especially surprising. As a port town, Astoria was noted especially for its nightlife. Toward the turn of the century, Astoria was the home of twelve churches and forty-two saloons, a ratio that was the inverse of most of the rest of Oregon. The brothel district was called Swilltown, and it was as alluring and spicy as anything in the Old West, since drinking, gambling, and prostitution were well tolerated by the city fathers as long as liquor licenses for the saloons brought in plenty of revenue.

In 1883 Astoria was a land of plenty, and the city was prosperous from the abundant salmon harvest. The citizens had money, and they restored their charred city without hesitation. By 1922 the city had grown respectable, trading its salty ways for more bourgeois pursuits, such as shipbuilding and salmon canning. By then many Scandinavians had settled in Astoria, especially the Finns. There were so many in the city that the street signs were printed in Finnish. Once, a young girl arrived from Finland after a long sea voyage to look for her only remaining relatives. Lost, orphaned, speaking no English, and alone in the world, not knowing if her relatives were even alive, she wandered from block to block, weeping. A Chinese taxi driver took pity on her and asked—in perfect Finnish—what he could do to help. She related her sad tale, and he said he knew just who her relatives were and how to find them. "Get in, and I'll take you there," he said. She stood, amazed, and asked him how in the world a man from China could speak Finnish so well. Simple, he replied, if you don't speak Finnish, you can't work in Astoria.

In 1922 central Astoria was a pretty, commercial district of

The Elks Building was destroyed in 1922 by Astoria's second great fire. This devastating blaze destroyed buildings that had been constructed after the 1833 fire. FROM THE COLLECTION OF ROXANN GESS SMITH

two- and three-story wooden Victorian buildings built after the 1883 fire. Shops and businesses occupied the ground floor, while the upper stories held apartments. A modern trolley system connected one end of town to the other. Astoria's streets were covered in asphalt so autos could travel them easily. But most of the buildings and even the very streets they rested on were built from the great Douglas fir trees surrounding the city. William Wotton, a fisherman and poet who grew up in Astoria, recalled that "at one time, in the early days, all downtown streets were on pilings. From the waterfront, up past Duane was all on piling, fir planking, three by twelves."

At 2:00 in the quiet early morning of December 8, a fire started somewhere in the business district of Astoria. It was a cold and dry night, with exceptionally low humidity, and the flames began to spread rapidly.

Frightened people poured into the empty streets, roused from sleep and ill clad for the cold winter's night. Some were clutching the few belongings they had managed to save. C. C. Pelton was fast asleep in his room at the Weinhard-Astoria Hotel—the height of luxury and the pride of Astoria—when he was startled out of a deep sleep. "I was awakened about 3:30 o'clock by a heavy pounding on my door and dressed immediately and went downstairs," he told the *Morning Oregonian*. Emerging into the night, he was surprised to see, in the red glare of the fire, a large crowd filling the streets, many of whom he recognized from the Weinhard-Astoria. He saw others who were staying in the surrounding hotels and lodging houses. At the Weinhard the evacuation was orderly—a policeman and a hotel attendant knocked on every door, double-checked every room, and forcibly aroused the heavy sleepers by breaking down the doors. Everyone was evacuated, but only about an hour after Pelton was awakened, he watched the beautiful hotel burn to the ground.

"When I came out onto the street at 3:30 o'clock," said Pelton, "two entire blocks had already been consumed and the fire was spreading rapidly." While evacuation efforts were successful, fighting the fire was another story. The firefighters vainly battled the fire, unable to make any progress in containing it. Because the water mains under the city had exploded in the heat of the fire, and then collapsed, the water pressure had disappeared. Their fire hoses were useless. The fire department lacked the sheer number of firefighters it would take to actively contain the fire. As the fire gained momentum, it reached gasoline tanks at garages and filling stations, producing terrifying explosions that punctuated the early morning.

The remains of the Weinhard Hotel and Astoria National Bank are shown in this picture of utter destruction. The town's financial losses added up to hundreds of millions of dollars. FROM THE COLLECTION OF ROXANN GESS SMITH

Crowds of spectators tried to help, but they also got in the way of the firefighters. Many people pitched in to help save belongings and inventories, but it was a hopeless task, for as soon as a store was emptied and its contents stacked safely out of harm's way 2 blocks down the street, sparks and debris would fly through the night and light more buildings on fire. Pelton said:

> With a number of others, I attempted to save the stock of a music store, which, when I first got out into the street, seemed far away from the path of the flames. We moved about thirty phonographs out of the building and a block away. A little while later, we were forced to carry the phonographs a block further.

And so it went throughout the night.

Not everyone got in the way—Astoria's telephone operators manned their switchboards in the telephone building until they were forced out by the flames. The chief operator, Miss J. Hitchcock, was on the telephone with a reporter from the *Portland Telegram*, describing the fire to him at 6 A.M. when she cut the reporter off, "Sorry, but we're ordered out; goodbye."

But had it not been for the vigilance of the operators, the fire could have taken a greater toll, for Portland sent extra firefighters when they heard that Astoria was in trouble. They were crucial in alerting the rest of Oregon that Astoria was in danger and needed help. At 10:15 a train arrived with relief firefighters, two steam pump engines, one gasoline engine, and 60,000 feet of hose. The imported water was aimed at the southern boundary of the fire so that it would not creep into the residential part of town. The firefighting team also began to dynamite the fire, which deprived it of oxygen. Even after the fire was officially out, firefighters dynamited more, just to be sure.

As H. H. Beaumont, a Portland firefighter, saw it:

> The Astoria firemen put up a game fight, but the cards were stacked against them. Once the fire got started, it ran along under the streets. The creosoted piles and the asphalt covering of the streets added fuel to the flames. It was impossible to get hose on the fires under the streets.

Not only the fuel, but the pilings themselves were a problem—they conducted oxygen to the fire, essentially acting as a gigantic chimney flue. It was a recipe for an inferno: dry wooden planks as the major fuel, asphalt and creosote as the fire starter, and tunnels under the fire to provide a rich source of oxygen. Even if the firefighters had had enough personnel and perfect equipment, they were up against difficult odds.

Especially troublesome, Beaumont reported, was "the lack of experienced firemen. The Astoria chief had considerable trouble in getting help. The people were sort of dazed—they stood around and looked on and didn't know how to fight fire." C. C. Pelton observed this as well, noting that "men, women, and children crowded the streets close to the flames, watching their property and belongings go up in smoke and unable to lift a hand, hindering, rather than aiding the work of fighting the fire."

As William Wotten recalled it:

> There wasn't anything anybody could do about it. The way the streets were built and laid out, if you were fighting one building in front of you, you looked around and saw a building behind you on fire. Dynamiting was all that stopped the fire.

Pelton guessed that by 7 A.M. that morning, about 18 blocks had burned. When the fire was finally contained at noon, 28 blocks had been destroyed.

Early rumors speculated that hundreds and hundreds had perished, but it turned out that the fire claimed just one life—the president of the Astoria Bank of Commerce. He also had an automobile dealership, the Staples Motor Company, and he died while pushing cars out of the company garage to keep them safe from the encroaching fire. That only one life was lost was lucky, especially considering the time of the fire.

Nonetheless, there was plenty of tragedy. Nearly 2,500 people were left homeless by the fire, and financial losses added up to hundreds of millions of dollars. Few Astorians were insured. The rates in the city were beyond the means of most people, due to the risk of fire associated with the town's wooden sidewalks.

Somehow the citizens of Astoria found the wherewithal to rebuild their city. They put in a new movie theater. They took out the apartments and put in modern storefronts. And most important, this time around, Astoria replaced the fir-planked streets with concrete.

CHAPTER 4

DANGEROUS SLOPES

The Mazamas on Coe Glacier

1927

The first recorded recreational mountain-climbing fatality in the United States occurred on Mount Hood, on July 12, 1896, when a man named Fredric Kirn was caught up in a rockslide and fell over a cliff to his death. Despite that, Mount Hood has always been an irresistible target for climbers, experienced and novice alike.

By 1927 Mount Hood was a hub of mountaineering activity. In spite of its dangers, it has always been a popular climb. Though it is tall, at 11,239 feet, it is not as technically challenging as many other glaciated peaks. It is also easy to get to, with a decent road being built in the early 1920s. Before the road, rich Portlanders would take the overnight sternwheeler from Portland to Hood River. Then they would take a stagecoach along a narrow wagon road to the Cloud Cap Inn. From there hardy souls would climb Mount Hood along Cooper Spur, while their less-ambitious friends would watch them from a comfortable spot at the inn. Today, there is a highway, and you can drive to Mount Hood in two hours from Portland.

Coe Glacier is considered Mount Hood's most dangerous climb, even with today's modern equipment. PHOTO TAKEN BY L. J. BAILEY, 1935. COURTESY NATIONAL SNOW AND ICE CENTER/WORLD DATA CENTER FOR GLACIOLOGY, BOULDER.

Mount Hood's popularity can be largely credited to its beauty and to the mountaineering club called the Mazamas, which is a derivative of a Native American word meaning "mountain goat." The Mazamas were the first of the major alpine clubs in the United States and its democratic, inclusive origins were reflected in its birth. In 1894, on June 12, an announcement in the *Morning Oregonian* read: "To Mountain Climbers and Lovers of Nature . . . it has been decided to meet on the summit of Mount Hood on the 19th of next month."

This invitation brought more than 300 mountain climbers and lovers of nature, men and women alike, to the mountain. The first group of climbers reached the summit by 8 A.M. on

July 19, and they were soon joined by 193 others. The Mazamas was formed by 105 of these climbers, and the club has been active in all aspects of mountaineering since then, teaching thousands of people to climb safely and enjoy the sport. Membership simply requires that one climb a glaciated peak.

Later, the Mazamas were joined by other clubs—for example, the Mountaineers in Washington, and in Oregon, the Crag Rats. The latter was formed in 1926 from a group of Hood River Valley friends who climbed together. They had helped out in several search-and-rescue operations, including returning a lost boy to his family. Reporters asked them the name of their group, and one of them, thinking of how his wife referred to them, answered, "The Crag Rats." In this way the Crag Rats became both a recreational club and experts in search-and-rescue work, and like the Mazamas, they are still in operation today.

As Mount Hood was the birthplace of the Mazamas, every year near July 19, they would organize a "birthday climb" up the mountain. In 1927 the date fell on July 17, a day that dawned fair. It was clear and beautiful in a way that only Oregon in July can be, with deep blue skies that go on forever and saturating, lemony sunlight. It was the perfect day to climb a mountain.

As a result of the beautiful weather and the birthday climb, Mount Hood was swarming with climbers struggling up the south-side glaciers and struggling up those on the north. The Crag Rats were busy practicing for a ski tournament. Other groups were on Cooper Spur and Eliot Glacier. But mostly, they were on Coe Glacier—which even today is thought to be Mount Hood's most treacherous, exciting, and difficult ice climb.

The climbing Mazamas had begun at 3 A.M.—all 103 of them. The hike was planned to proceed from the American

Legion camp near Cloud Cap Inn, over the summit, and then on to the alpine village of Government Camp. A celebration dinner was scheduled for 4 P.M., and families and friends were watching the group from the Cloud Cap Inn, which had a fine view of the glacier. Some were trading heliograph signals between the inn and Coe Glacier.

The climbers had approached Coe from the Sunshine Trail. The alternative, the more popular Cooper Spur Trail, was examined the week before and thought to be unsafe, and the leader of the Mazamas, Judge Stadter of Portland, didn't want to take any chances. The annual climb was open to everyone, beginners and expert climbers alike, so they had to make allowances for different levels of experience—as well as the sheer number of climbers participating. A significant number had never before climbed anything, so the Mazamas leaders were meticulous in their preparations. They made sure everyone had the proper equipment and checked their boots and ropes. They were thorough in teaching them how to use the alpenstock—an iron-painted climbing staff—and where to place their feet.

And so it was that at 2 P.M., 103 climbers, men and women, novice and expert, were roped together in groups of ten or so, picking their way across the ice of Coe Glacier. On the way up they had a narrow escape at the west side of Eliot Glacier. A small avalanche had tumbled down the mountain and nearly swept the party along with it, knocking one person down. They managed to stay out of harm's way, yet it gave the climbers pause.

Judge Stadter, together with two fellow Mazamas, had scaled the mountain the week before to lay out the best route. They had never tried, as a group, to ascend Mount Hood via the

Sunshine Trail, but while parts of the upper glacier seemed treacherous, they decided that, with expert guidance and constant vigilance, this route could be achieved.

The guides monitored the progress of the climbers. They were about an hour away from the summit when they stopped for a little rest. All at once, the line of climbers broke as two members of the third party began to slide down the ice. It seemed that their alpenstocks had slipped, and they were dragging the rest of the party with them. One by one, the other climbers were pulled away. They tried to stay themselves as they fell by thrusting their alpenstocks into the snow. The experienced climbers, including Dr. Stanton Stryker, a Portland dentist and long-time Mazama, were each able to get a firm hold several times, only to be dragged away by the whiplike motion of the line—one end, then the other. The group skidded 200 yards out of control to their doom. Alarmed bystanders—their fellow climbers, as well as those at the Cloud Cap Inn—and the climbers themselves could all see they were headed straight for a crevasse. And one by one, with terrible screams, they dropped over its edge, their cries echoing across the mountain.

At once, the guides and more experienced climbers slid down the slope after them. Perley Payton was the first to reach the edge and what he saw must have been hopeful, for he yelled, "Are any of you hurt?"

"Yes we are—badly," was the reply.

Then others threw down their axes and cast off their ropes and slid down to the edge of the crevasse. At the edge the line of the slope was slightly extended over the crevasse, slowing down the descent. The victims were lying in soft snow 20 feet below, on a bench of rock.

As Judge Stadter arrived on the scene, Payton started down the mountain to seek help. Judge Stadter and another Mazama, Merle Manley, hurried down the slope and tried to find an approach to the crevasse from the other side to tend the injured. From this approach they pulled the injured climbers back from the soft snow at the seam of the crevasse, for if it gave way, it would have thrown them down 100 more feet to certain death.

But death was still a worry. When the climbers arrived at the scene of the accident, they saw a pile of bodies tangled up in the snow. Clem Blakney, a guide who had assisted many climbing parties' ascent to the top, pulled Mary Mallory of Portland, whose right ankle had a compound fracture, out from the snarl of people, gear, and rope. But he could do little for Dr. Stryker, who had fallen on an alpenstock, piercing his body through. Dr. Stryker had tried desperately to stave off his party's fall and had done everything he could to slow it down. Blakney removed him from the cluster, withdrawing the alpenstock from his side, but Stryker was losing consciousness fast, and it didn't require a doctor to see that he had little time.

The rescue work was organized by the Mazamas who had remained at Cloud Cap; they set about alerting doctors and nurses in the nearest town, Hood River. And they were assisted by the Crag Rats, who had witnessed the entire accident. The Crag Rats supplied a stretcher and first-aid kit. Two small sleds that some climbers were planning to use on their descent were commandeered to use to bring down the injured. Rescuers also fashioned stretchers from packs, coats, and alpenstocks, and horses were brought in. It took several hours for them to carry the injured climbers safely off the mountain. Four could walk out, but the rest had to be transported, and descending a glacier on Mount Hood is dangerous under the best of conditions. Dr. Stryker had lost consciousness and was only about half a mile from where he landed before he died.

The remaining climbers did their best to get out of the way when they saw they would not be of use. They organized themselves, crested the summit, and then descended to Government Camp.

After this accident the Mazamas became renowned for their conservative approach to climbing and safety. They were already careful, but now they undertook detailed studies of technique, equipment, geology, personal characteristics, the characteristics of ice and snow, and so on, in order to better prepare for future climbs.

That only one person died in this dramatic incident was almost miraculous. The victims were largely saved by the shape of the land they slid over, since the angle broke their speed. Years later, however, five Mazamas would die in a similar accident. On a Sunday in June 1981, a party of sixteen climbers fell 2,000 feet down Eliot Glacier when one rope team lost its footing, crashing into the other teams in a "zipper" fall. Indeed, almost one hundred people have died climbing or hiking Mount Hood since 1896 when Fredric Kirn gave his life to the mountain.

More than 10,000 people climb Mount Hood every year. Many years see the death of at least one person. Climbers today may have state-of-the-art polar equipment, cell phones, and years of training, but one thing that hasn't changed is the risk of a slight misstep. But if the risk isn't there, neither is the challenge.

C H A P T E R 5

"JUST ONE MORE LOG"

The Tillamook Burn

1933

The Wilson River Highway is a green, sleepy highway. Lined with fir, spruce, alder, and maple trees, it connects the coastal town of Tillamook, Oregon, with the city of Portland. In July 1933 the highway was a green, sleepy old stagecoach road, barely one lane wide. By September it was a trail of ash 2 feet deep in a ghost forest with no sign of life.

Oregon has a well-deserved reputation for rain, but summers are usually warm and dry—even hot. July and August may see only a trace of rain, or none at all. Lawns go brown and everyone complains of the drying heat. That's the sign of fire weather: After weeks of little rain, a heat wave settles in to absorb any remaining moisture that might be locked in plant or earth. It was just such a summer in 1933. That August, the beautiful, ancient Tillamook forest caught fire, ultimately burning 311,000 acres of timberland that had not seen such a fire in 400 years. And that was just the first fire.

According to Oregon lore, the fire began on the afternoon of August 14, at the Gales Creek logging camp in western Oregon. Gales Creek was a small settlement in the Tillamook forest, just west of the town of Forest Grove, between the Oregon coast and Portland. In 1933 the Tillamook forest was renowned for being the best stand of virgin timber remaining in the United States, and it was vital to the economy of the state. The Great Depression was beginning to ease, and for the first time in years, people were beginning to build again. Demand had increased for the sturdy old-growth timber that the Tillamook forest provided. Men who had been out of work were hired by logging companies and were finally bringing paychecks home.

On August 14, 1933, the Gales Creek Logging Company was going full bore. The lumbermen had just resumed their work after lunch, and they were getting ready to haul a giant Douglas fir out of the underbrush. But a runner from the fire-watching authorities arrived, winded and sweaty, on an urgent errand. He told the men at Gales Creek to stop: "You'll have a fire on your hands." And stop they did—for a moment. The men operating the heavy equipment paused. The boss stopped and thought for a moment. He agreed. They would stop. But, he said, just one more log.

August 14 was a hot, dry day in a hot, dry summer. The humidity that day was recorded at 22 percent. The dry dust of the forest floor was deep and clung to the loggers' boots, invading every crevice. Oregon governor Julius Meier had already closed the state-owned forests to logging. But he had no jurisdiction over the vast ranges of privately held forest that made up the Tillamook forest. All he could do was ask the logging company to please stop.

What happened next was not totally clear, and accounts vary. Some writers say that after the order was given to load the last giant log, a spark was thrown as the tree was dragged over the crumbling and desiccated windfall that lined the forest floor. Others say it was the friction of a thick cable against a dry

The 1933 forest fire known as the Tillamook Burn blazed from August 14 until the rain came on September 5. LIBRARY OF CONGRESS PHOTO, LC-USF34-070682-D

stump. What is clear is that the spark generated by the last log ignited the Tillamook Burn.

The loggers in the Gales Creek camp sounded the alarm, and "Fire!" was the rallying cry up and down the valley. Men seized their axes and shovels in an attempt to extinguish the fire. But their efforts were thwarted by the hot winds that blew sparks throughout the forest and fueled the fire. In 1933 there were few ways to reach a fire in the Tillamook forest. The forest lies in a steep, mountainous area, much of which is remote. There were no fire roads to bring in people and equipment where they were needed most. Communication was difficult because radio and telephone access were limited. Smoke jumpers were not available because the Russians hadn't invented them yet. So at least in the beginning, the only way to battle the fire was to use shovels, picks, and axes to try to smother it, and that meant getting to the fire before the wind did. But shortly after the first wisp of smoke puffed into the sky, the flames were leaping up an old snag, and from there, cinders flew half a mile with the winds, igniting the slash—the dead branches and leaves left over from logging—across Gales Creek Canyon. There was no hope of smothering the fire now. All the loggers could do was to dig firebreaks to deprive the fire of new fuel.

A dry summer, a spell of heat, and low humidity are danger signs for foresters, and when the wind blows in from the east, those who make their living from the land are on constant watch. When the winds gathered strength on August 15, the men fighting the fire at Gales Creek knew how to read those signs. The temperature reached 104, more than ten degrees hotter than the day before. The humidity had dropped, and worst of all, fierce east winds began to rush down from the Cascades, picking up speed as they blew over the valleys. The winds were what everyone feared. They pushed the fire deep into the forest, into stands of giant trees, well over 100 feet tall. This was a dire turn of fate, for if the fire reached these tallest trees, it would crown, lighting the tops of those trees like torches. The crowning trees would fling fiery debris into the forest for miles in every direction, making the fire impossible to control.

Sure enough, on August 15, the fire crowned, with all its dreadful consequences. By late afternoon, fire watchers were reporting eleven small "spot" fires, and a worrisome large one 15 miles south of the Gales Creek fire, near the Wilson River.

This latter fire took root and quickly grew larger than the fire that produced it.

The firefighting corps had also grown. Loggers were joined by local firemen, men from the Civilian Conservation Corps, farmers, and other volunteers. Fresh crews were brought in order to work around the clock, for the only chance they had was to gain enough time to dig breaks around the two fires. But this would not be easy—it was hot, dirty, relentless work, and the fires were moving fast. The heat from the fire was so great that the firefighters had to plunge their tools in streams to cool them enough to be able to hold them.

The firefighters dug break after break. And the fires crowned again and again, exploding all around the firefighters and forcing them to retreat. All across the Willamette Valley, Oregonians were beginning to notice the thick smoke emanating from the Oregon Coast Range. That night, the skies glowed red.

But there were signs of hope. While the Wilson Creek fire was yet raging, firefighters seemed to be progressing against the Gales Creek fire. They were helped by new recruits, as well as by the temperature, which had dropped twenty degrees; the humidity, which was much higher; and the east wind's ceasing to blow. By August 17, 600 men were fighting the fire, and by August 18, there were more than 1,000. The logging town of Forest Grove became the central staging ground, with the U.S. Army called in to distribute food and equipment and organize the firefighters. The weather grew even more promising as a mist dampened the air. Evolving evacuation plans for Forest Grove were put on hold. For the next three days, firefighting efforts ran round the clock, and the fire was contained at 20,000 acres. At last, it seemed, the fire was under control, almost a week after it had begun.

And but for the east wind, it would have been. On August 20, however, the east wind awoke from its slumber and roared back over the Willamette Valley. Fed by the wind, the fire leapt to 40,000 acres, destroying in moments two firefighting camps, with the workers barely escaping. Now it wasn't simply a job for the firefighters. Throughout the region everyone was on constant fire watch—men, women, and children were all called to smother the smoldering coals that endangered pasturelands, farms, and homes. People's eyes and nostrils stung from the smoke. In the town of Forest Grove, which was the largest community threatened by the fire, you could feel the fire's heat.

The fire blazed on. The smoke was so thick that it was impossible to see where the fire was going. That the fire was burning in ever more remote and difficult terrain struck fear into hearts across western Oregon. There was neither a way to stop the fire nor a way to gauge where it would next erupt. All the towns, farms, ranches, and woodland homesteads in the region were at risk. The fire had jumped both banks of the Wilson River and was burning out of control, fast. Amazingly, however, in some parts of the Tillamook forest, logging operations were still going on, and on August 22, machinery sparked yet another blaze. This fire began on Mount Trask, at the Cadwalander and Davis Mill, south of the Gales Creek fire. Within moments the mill was burned to the ground, and the fire was sent raging into the forest.

Farther north, the lookout who had first reported the Gales Creek fire called headquarters to alert them he was leaving his post—he expected it to be consumed shortly, since the fire was encroaching South Saddle Mountain. The Southern Pacific Railroad company stopped passenger service up and down the coast, instead devoting all its time to securing its tracks. They were concerned that the fire would spread west toward the Pacific and wanted to soak down the tracks so they wouldn't burn. The Pacific Telephone and Telegraph Company was worried that the Trask fire would incinerate their lines to the town of Tillamook on the coast. And the truck drivers who were hauling supplies to the fire lines were worried for their survival. As the fire raged all along the roads, it threw down burning trees, and its heat was so intense that it blistered the paint on the trucks and scorched their wooden beds.

Throughout the day on August 22, new spot fires were reported throughout the region. By nightfall it appeared that the spot fires were joining forces. But on August 23, the wind died down and fog rolled in. The temperature fell to fifty-two degrees. The major threats—the Wilson River and Trask fires—suddenly seemed conquerable. In a more hopeful mood, people set about repairing phone lines and other equipment that the fire had destroyed. But August 24 dawned hot and dry, the humidity falling to its lowest level of the summer. Fire wardens told all the towns and villages, fire crews, farmers, and ranchers on the south and west sides of the fire to evacuate—immediately.

That afternoon, the fire exploded into the air after it hit a stand of old-growth trees 250 feet tall. Eighteen miles of solid flame stretched across the Tillamook forest. This wall created a cloud of smoke that stretched 40 miles across. As the hot air rushing toward the heavens drew fresh, oxygen-rich air into the fire, it generated a cyclone of flame that sucked up all the smaller fires, catapulting giant trees out of the earth and hurling them for miles in every direction.

The effects were immense. The fire sped through the forest, devouring 166 acres per minute. Spot fires were ignited throughout four counties. Governor Meier ordered all logging to stop. Animals poured out of the forest. A young firefighter with the Civilian Conservation Corps, Frank Palmer, was crushed and killed when a burning snag fell on him, and another man with him was terribly injured. Ships 500 miles at sea were showered with flaming debris. The smoke climbed 8 miles into the air, visible even to tourists at Yellowstone National Park. Thick ash rained down upon the coastal towns of Oregon—in Tillamook, Garibaldi, Wheeler, Nehalem—and on the farms and towns of the Willamette Valley. The fire burned within a mile of Forest Grove. Smaller villages were thought to be doomed, cut off from the world as their bridges burned. Portland was hidden by smoke. It was so dark that cars had their headlights on during the day. In some places visibility dropped to 100 feet. Chickens were reported to roost at noon, and cows could not reach their pastures to graze because 3 feet of ash lay upon them.

In the midst of this apocalypse, however, emerged some good news. The little town of Elsie was among those reported lost, but the women and children who remained there while the men were on the fire lines had successfully defended it against the blaze with wet sacks and sheer vigilance in putting out sparks. Wet cloth sacks were the only recourse many people had in the absence of sprinkler systems or hoses. Fires often interfere with water pressure, so even if such things had been available, there was no guarantee they would have worked. Instead, people soaked cloth in ash-muddied streams and creeks—and kept alert.

Likewise, along the Wilson River a ranger station was saved by the hard work of a crew of ten. One of these was a high school student, Wilfred Pullem. All through the night, he filled pans of water from a low spring so the men could soak their sacks and keep the fire from destroying the building—which was about all firefighters could do at this point. Across the reach of the burn, they fought to save the structures that they could and to make sure people were safe from the flames. One woman who lived on the Trask River defied the evacuation order and stayed with her two-year-old on her homestead throughout the fire. The baby wandered outside as the mother was doing her chores. When the mother went outside after her, she saw the child about to be set upon by a large bear. She screamed. Her dog barked. Together they rushed the bear, who ran back to the smoking forest, evidently choosing the danger of fire over the threat presented by an angry mother.

On August 27, the winds once again died down and the temperatures dropped as coastal fog rolled in. Smoke lay thick in the Willamette Valley and enshrouded Portland, but the fire was slowing as the weather began to turn. On September 5, it began to rain heavily for days, and the rain finally contained the Tillamook Burn. In the final assessment, 311,000 acres had burned—240,000 of them between August 24 and 25. And those totals do not include the 60,000 acres burned in another fire near the small town of Vernonia, nor the 40,000-acre fire that had consumed fine timber near Astoria.

For Oregonians the Tillamook Burn was a deep blow. Accounts from the time document the loss in stark economic terms: Twelve billion board feet of timber were lost, representing hundreds of jobs, timber that would have kept Portland sawmills busily working for thirty years and built more than a million houses. For every dollar the timber owners lost, five dollars were lost to the local economy. Some money was made by salvaging what usable timber could be found—though scouters looking for salvage logs found a hulking, giant fir snag still smoldering a year after the fire was contained—but it would be decades before the area recovered economically. Even worse, the fires returned with precision, every six years until 1951. In 1939, 190,000 acres burned in a fire that was also triggered by logging. In 1945, 180,000 acres burned, and in 1951, another 32,000. All of these fires covered the same areas as the previous ones, attacking the remaining pockets of forest and the logged-off salvage operations.

The 1945 fire was the one that finally stirred the public to do something. The fire started several months after the Japanese had tried to use incendiary bombs to burn Oregon's forests, sending nearly 70,000 toward the West Coast of the United States. Of these 1,000 reached their targets. They did little damage to the forests, but one did kill six people in southern Oregon, near Bly—the only war-related deaths on the continental United States. Understandably, then, the 1945 burn was deeply unsettling to Oregonians. The fire began—no one knows how—on July 10, and it burned steadily for more than a month. The fires were covered with intense interest by the newspapers, supplanted only by news of the dropping of the atom bomb on Hiroshima and the subsequent surrender of Japan.

After the 1945 burn, the Tillamook forest became a kind of laboratory for policy and research on reforestation. After a protracted political battle, the voters narrowly approved a bond measure to purchase the lands affected by the fire. Oregon's citizens, rather than logging companies, now owned the forest, and they were determined to replant it. A great community effort ensued. Even schoolchildren were involved. From throughout the state they arrived in buses, trowels in hand, to do their part.

Most of the land, however, was reforested by determined professionals, who learned much about how to manage a forest, about the requirements of trees for soil and elevation, about the effects of climate, about controlling the mice and deer who loved to eat the baby trees, and about how best to plant seedlings. They tried various strategies, including mimicking the wind by dropping seeds from airplanes, but eventually settled on hand planting.

Their work paid off. In 1973, forty years after the first fire, the Tillamook Burn was officially rechristened as the Tillamook State Forest, and in 1983 the first trees were ready for logging. The area is now a multiuse forest, with beautiful parks and trails, logging activity, and protected wilderness zones. Along the Wilson River Highway, about 20 miles east of Tillamook, you'll find a historic marker in homage to the Tillamook Burn, to the men and women who fought it, to the Oregonians who reforested it. But the marker is also an homage to the great resilience of the forest itself, independent of human hands, and its cycle of destruction and renewal. Driving down the Wilson River Highway now, bordered as it is by thick green trees, you'd never know it was once devastated by a terrible fire. But the appearance of forests is deceiving, and their nature makes it likely—inevitable—that the Tillamook forest will burn again.

CHAPTER 6

HERE TODAY, GONE TOMORROW

The Vanport Flood

1948

In the north part of Portland is a series of beautiful parks, sports fields, golf courses, and shopping malls that occupy a low-lying, riverside plain. On a typical Sunday in May, there you might find hundreds of children playing in soccer tournaments, fans cheering at racetrack events, and golfers watching herons and eagles as they wait for their partners to drive the ball. Many of those soccer players and sports fans and golfers would be surprised to learn that underneath their feet are the remains of a once-thriving town that was built by people in a matter of weeks and destroyed a few years later by a flood, in a matter of hours.

That town was Vanport. It was assembled in 1943 to house workers who had poured into Portland from all across the United States to build ships for the U.S. Navy during World War II. The Kaiser Shipbuilding Company was furiously building Liberty ships for the war effort—by September 1942 they could build one of these sturdy, practical ships in about two weeks, about 75 percent faster than anyone had ever done it before. Workers were on the assembly line twenty-four hours a day. But to achieve this pace of production, Kaiser needed a lot of workers. And Portland simply did not have enough of them.

Yet Portland received the new arrivals with ambivalence. To have all of these workers coming to town seemed a mixed blessing to the city authorities. On the one hand, it was good for the economy. On the other, it was a disruptive change. Suddenly, the city was overflowing with people who had no place to live. They were given trailers and housed in dormitories, but these were only temporary solutions. Not only were there a lot of workers, but many of them were African Americans, and Portland—and Oregon as a whole—was not friendly to them. The city authorities, in particular the Housing Authority of Portland, were worried that if they built permanent housing, then the African-American workers might decide to stay.

Portland already had a track record of exclusionary housing policies. The city had voted in 1938 to reject federally funded housing designed to help people still suffering from the Great Depression because voters thought it would lower property values. Now, even faced with severe housing shortages, the city government balked. The Housing Authority of Portland was beholden to special interests, such as local landlords, the Realty Board, and the real estate industry in general, who wanted to maximize their profits, rather than provide housing for factory workers. So the city authorities dragged their feet, building only about 5,000 housing units when nearly 40,000 were needed.

Henry Kaiser couldn't wait for the city fathers to become more enlightened. He had ships to build. He went around the Housing Authority of Portland and, using the same talent that allowed him to reduce the time it took to build a warship, built the city of Vanport, just outside the city limits. Vanport was built on a low plain surrounded by huge dikes that kept out the waters of the Columbia, the Columbia Slough, and Smith Lake.

It featured nearly 10,000 apartments, five grade schools, six child-care centers (open twenty-four hours, just like the ship factories), three fire stations, a library, a movie theater, a post office, grocery stores, a hospital—in fact it was pretty much a complete town. Ten thousand people were living there by March of 1943, and by the end of the war, it had 40,000 residents.

By May 1948, however, the war was over and the shipyards were quiet. Vanport had always been looked at askance by the rest of Portland, and for a time after the war, its reputation dipped even further. As the shipbuilding factory shut down production, job losses led to some crime and delinquency, and a high percentage of Vanport's declining number of residents were on welfare. But by 1948 Vanport had become desirable once more. The community was recovering, and a major reason was that many liked its proximity to Vanport College, an extension of Oregon State University that was very popular for veterans on the GI Bill. In 1948 about 18,500 people lived in the city, which provided sorely needed housing for veterans and their families, and even for the beloved Portland Beavers baseball team. Community involvement and morale were improving. Small businesses were opening. More people were moving in than moving out. Yet to the rest of Portland, Vanport retained a reputation of being a crime-ridden federal housing project full of black people who had no respect for property or law.

May is typically a beautiful month in Oregon. But 1948 had seen a very snowy winter in the Cascades, and that year, May was both warm and rainy. The Columbia River, which flowed alongside Vanport, brought rain and snowmelt from throughout all of the Northwest—seven states in all, as well as British Columbia—to the Pacific. Rivers from the Canadian Rockies, rivers from Idaho and Montana, such as the Kootenai and Flathead, the Clearwater and Salmon, contributed to the surge of runoff. Earlier that spring, the weather had been drier and cooler than usual, so the snowpack in the mountains had not melted much by the end of May, and there was a lot of it. Officials began their flood watch in late May, for the Columbia was rising fast.

On May 25, the Housing Authority of Portland began organizing patrols of the dikes that surrounded the town, just in case. The Army Corps of Engineers told the Housing Authority that the dikes were very sound and likely to withstand any high water. Besides, they had easily withstood a flood two years prior, in 1946.

To the citizens of Vanport, the message was clear: You are safe. At 4 A.M. on Sunday, May 28, authorities put under the door of every Vanport residence a reassuring letter that explained that flooding was unlikely, but just in case, it gave instructions for evacuating. It stated that sirens would be sounded. And it concluded with this message:

> REMEMBER:
> DIKES ARE SAFE AT PRESENT.
> YOU WILL BE WARNED IF NECESSARY.
> YOU WILL HAVE TIME TO LEAVE.
> DON'T GET EXCITED.

The morning dawned fair and bright. It was warm, so many residents decided to spend this Sunday at the coast or in Portland. But the Red Cross, the sheriff, and the Housing Authority were preparing for disaster. The Columbia River flood gauge marked the river at 28 feet, 13 feet above flood level—and 15 feet above the ground level of Vanport. They waited to see if the dikes would hold.

When the break came, it was not where they thought it would be. It was not at the dikes along the Columbia or even along the Slough. It was the mighty railroad dike that separated Vanport from Smith Lake. And it was mighty indeed: 125 feet across at the base and 75 across at the top. Everyone had assumed that it was the strongest dike, that nothing could breach it, because it was so massive. Moreover, it was the farthest dike from the flooding river. And the waters had not risen over the top—they were 17 feet below the top of the railroad.

Yet the railroad dike was the first to collapse, and it happened suddenly—a 6-foot hole quickly grew to 60 and then 500 feet. A man named Calvin Hubert watched it happen; he was flying his plane above the railroad tracks. At 4:17 that afternoon, the water broke through, pushing a 10-foot wave through the breach, which sent cars spinning and scattering and knocked buildings off their foundations within minutes. Once the water broke through the dike, it collided with the water in the many sloughs that lay within Vanport itself. People witnessed waves 50 feet high as the flood waters dramatically flushed into the standing water. Luckily, however, the sloughs also slowed the flooding down, absorbing much of the flood like a sponge. This meant that the water rose steadily but slowly enough that people could sound the alarm.

It was not the promised sirens, but students and faculty at Vanport College who first alerted residents. They had come in on this Memorial Day–weekend Sunday to secure their research and other important papers and personal belongings, but when the moment came, they abandoned their things to spread through neighborhood after neighborhood to sound the alarm. Meanwhile, the sheriff's office had been warned, and they sent every bus and taxi they could reach to Vanport to assist with the evacuation.

The sloughs absorbed a lot of the flood, but after they filled up, Vanport lay covered by a sheet of standing water, temporarily dammed by the remaining dikes. Power to the city was lost at 4:50. By 5:00 P.M. the flood had started to move again, sending the surging water to destroy whatever was in its path. Even worse, now the Willamette River, which winds through Portland but did not directly border Vanport, got in on the action. Its flood gauge actually dipped as its waters began to drain into lowlands surrounding the town and then through the breaches in the dikes. Vanport was filling up like a bowl.

There was only one road out of Vanport; it led to Denver Avenue and the east dike, which seemed to be holding for now. As the waters rushed in, the people of Vanport began to rush out, heading for the high east dike. The promised sirens came very late. People grabbed what belongings they could and tried to get out as fast as possible. The early fleers could leave by car, but since there was but one road out, the traffic was soon gridlocked. As the waters rose most people had to abandon their cars. Eyewitness accounts of the evacuation are inconsistent, but three universal themes stand out: the concern for children, the eerie silence, and the lack of panic. Everyone seemed to temporarily forget their differences and just tried to get one another out.

When the water got too deep for the cars that remained—which was most of them—people had to grab what belongings they could and hike out. To assist those who had to wade through water to safety, people formed chains or found ropes; to rescue those who could not walk out, they used boats. At first those who were trapped in apartments had to jump precariously into these boats, but as the waters rose, they found they could just step out of the window. One man, apparently very drunk, dove out of a boat and swam to an apartment building—and to an unknown fate. One couple had to be chopped out of a house that had leaned so far over that its doors and windows were inaccessible. Many people climbed onto roofs. Others escaped by clinging to, or even riding on, boards, mattresses, and whatever else they could find. The water was hazardous, filled with uprooted telephone poles and other large debris—including the apartment buildings themselves, most of which were pushed off their foundations, floating like giant houseboats throughout the town. Their pace was fortuitously slow, however, so many people were rescued from the second stories of these buildings even as they were floating along.

Searches organized by Sheriff Pratt and the National Guard (which had been immediately deployed by the governor) continued into the evening, rescuing families trapped in apartments and other buildings. The National Guard went all through the city in their amphibious "buffalo" trucks to search for survivors and bodies. The very thing that made Vanport dangerous—that it was contained within the walls of the dikes—also was an asset when it came to search and rescue. It was easy to find all the buildings and houses. By 9 P.M. everyone seemed to be out and not a single body had been found.

The next day, the search continued. Rescuers did find tableaux of sudden departures: an uncarved roast on a dining-room table, a newspaper opened to headlines declaring that the flood crest was due on Tuesday. But they found no bodies.

Indeed, the first known death did not occur until 9:30 P.M. on Monday. The Denver Avenue dike had thus far held, but the waters were rising against it fast. All day Monday, about one hundred workers shored up the dike, and it seemed that it would hold. But at 9:30 a Portland General Electric worker was killed when his car was caught in a new breach in the road, a gap that rapidly grew to 500 feet wide. It gave the apartment buildings somewhere to go, and they floated through the breach, alighting in the area just east of Vanport.

As predicted, the Columbia River crested on Tuesday, at 30.2 feet, and the floodwaters began to recede. Now the real work began.

There's a lot to be discouraged about in this life, but helping out in times of disaster seems to be in the DNA of Americans, and in the aftermath of the Vanport flood, this was especially true. White Portlanders opened their homes to black ones, money poured in from across the state and eventually the nation, flood survivors were efficiently organized by the National Guard and the Red Cross. On Sunday night schools were set up as temporary shelters, but by Tuesday they were no longer needed.

Typically, however, rescue efforts were also hampered by absurd bureaucratic regulations. Sheriff Pratt, who was a wise, practical, and efficient sort of person, thought that officially marked boats would be useful for the search-and-rescue mission. Naturally, he thought the Coast Guard might be willing to pitch in. So he went up to their local headquarters along the Columbia. No one was there. Neither were their boats. Sheriff Pratt eventually found the Coast Guard, along with their boats, at the Broadmoor Golf Course. The men were lying around not helping. Sheriff Pratt found this irritating. A Coast Guard officer explained that their regulations did not permit them to help out local police. Later on, the Coast Guard did put in appearance, finding one body and then not taking it to the coroner's depot, where it was supposed to go. Pratt generously blamed bureaucratic processes rather than the individual officers.

Based on what his deputies and he himself saw, as well as the work by the National Guard, Sheriff Pratt predicted fewer than twenty-five fatalities, for which he was openly mocked. Rumors were flying. Many claimed to have seen a busload of children trapped and sinking. Another rumor had it that a group of children had drowned in the theater. Others believed that, to avoid bad publicity for the upcoming annual Rose Festival, authorities had hidden 600 bodies in an ice storage facility. Still others believed that bodies had been loaded onto freighters bound for Japan, to be returned later as dead soldiers, so authorities could avoid liability for the flood. Even officials contributed, stating that the lower floors of apartment buildings were clogged with drowned humanity or speculating that hundreds of bodies were washed to sea with the flood. These rumors, and others, had just enough plausibility to persist—some of them for many years. For hadn't the residents been repeatedly assured that they were safe? And when all was said and done, didn't the people of Portland want Vanport to go away? Did it not have a reputation for crime and poverty? Perhaps the dike was deliberately breached to wash it away.

In reality the low number of deaths likely owed itself to the fact that the flood occurred on Memorial Day weekend, when many were away from home; to the fact that it was a Sunday, when businesses were closed; to the fact that the Vanport hospital had been moved on May 1 to Vancouver, Washington; and to the fact that the floodwaters were first absorbed by the sloughs, slowing the flood down by forty-five minutes and allowing people to get out in time. Still, the low number of casualties is remarkable. The official record was eventually set at fifteen, with an acknowledgment that there may have been a few others who could not be accounted for.

Even though the number of deaths was low, the survivors were in for a woeful time. At first there was open weeping as relatives and friends sought for one another in the confusion. People had lost everything and were desperate. And then there was the problem of where they would go. The very problem Vanport was built to address now reasserted itself with a vengeance—one that would play itself out over years of legal battles over liability and reparations, and one that in the end the people of Vanport lost.

Eventually, the city of Portland absorbed the residents of Vanport, as well as its institutions, and became the better for it. The Kaiser-built health clinic became Kaiser Permanente. Vanport College became Portland State University. And the people of Vanport became the citizens of Portland, contributing their experience to the vitality, creativity, and accomplishments of that city—as well as to a native mistrust of government officials.

C H A P T E R 7

ARCTIC ILLUSIONS

Three Blizzards

1950

It used to be—150 years ago—that in winter, you could ice skate from Portland all the way up to Oregon City on a frozen Willamette River. The Columbia, too, would freeze regularly. It was cold. But like everything else, the weather has gotten easier in modern times. It's not that Oregon doesn't have snow: We have mountains, after all, and eastern Oregon enjoys beautifully snowy winters. There, snow means business—the winter sports business—and one that is for the most part confined to higher elevations. But in the western half of the state, where the majority of people live, we haven't had snowy winters for a long time.

But January 1950 was snowy. Throughout the state a relentless series of three storms delivered record snowfall. That year, Crater Lake, Oregon, would accumulate 903 inches of snow, with 136 of those inches in January. That month, the dam at Detroit Lake received 122 inches of snow, the Cottage Grove dam 121 inches, and the Portland airport—at sea level—41 inches. Downtown, residents struggled with 33 inches of snow. Eugene had 36, Corvallis 52, and Clatskanie, more than 68. Across the state snowfall beat all records in the sixty years that had been officially kept: Pendleton, in eastern Oregon, 42 inches; the Dalles, on the Columbia River, 76. That January, 224 inches of snow fell at Timberline Lodge on Mount Hood.

Most of the snow fell from January 9 through January 18. In the beginning the snow was a welcome diversion. Newspapers were filled with cheerful accounts of frolicking schoolchildren enjoying their enforced vacations. But as the days dragged on, Oregonians grew weary of the unabated storms. January 13 was the worst—a severe blizzard that stranded motorists and closed every highway. On January 18, the blizzard turned into an ice storm, requiring motorists to be rescued by trains. The average daily low for the month was twenty-one degrees, and twice, in Portland, the temperature dropped below zero. In Salem, the thermometer dropped to ten below zero.

On January 13, cold air swept down from the plains of western Canada, which had been enduring Arctic weather for five weeks. At the same time a large storm from the Gulf of Alaska was moving south as well, reaching the mouth of the Columbia River and blowing inland. The result: a great blizzard.

The most spectacular effects of the blizzard were along the Columbia Gorge. Cars traveling down the pavement—which was glazed with several inches of ice—were blown off the road by the winds. One driver, attempting to pilot a flatbed truck, said, "I was going along okay, keeping in the road by watching power poles on the roadside. Then I couldn't see any poles. And the next thing, I was in the ditch."

Weather fronts along the Columbia Gorge regularly spill into the eastern parts of Portland, and this weather affected that area particularly. From Park Rose all the way to Troutdale, a stretch of 10 miles, more than thirty-five cars and trucks were stalled on the highway. Along the stretch of highway to Corbett, 10 miles east of Troutdale, there were at least seventy-five more stalled vehicles. The road there is just at the level of the Columbia, and it was cold, windy, and icy. Still farther east, an avalanche had cut off the town of Wyeth, east of Cascade Locks. Twenty truck drivers had parked their trucks alongside the road near Troutdale and headed for safety. More than 500 cars and trucks were thought to be stranded, but nobody really knew the exact number.

Snowplows were running endlessly, but it didn't keep the highway clear, and their progress was slow. For one thing the snow would simply blow in behind the already plowed road. For another the cars following the plows would slide and spin and stall. Cars without chains were particularly vulnerable. They would spin out and then block the other cars behind them, over and over. Eventually, the snowplows surrendered to the snowy conditions and simply stopped, 4 miles east of Troutdale.

One driver, H. A. Williams, told the *Oregonian* that it was the worst storm he had ever driven in. He had been on his way home to Portland from Madras, in central Oregon. Luckily, Williams followed a snowplow from Madras to Government Camp, along Highway 26. But it was an arduous journey, nevertheless. His car windows were so thick with frost that he couldn't see, except through a tiny opening in the windshield that he worked frantically to keep clear. Through this small opening he observed many stranded vehicles. At Government Camp he saw four freight trucks with large fires beside them, which the drivers had built to thaw the brakes of the trucks before they attempted to make the long descent into town.

All across the state branches fell, trees toppled, buildings collapsed, power lines wilted under the weight of ice. Pendleton recorded temperatures of minus four degrees, and La

Grand, minus five. At the University of Oregon, a portable classroom was crushed when a tall old fir tree fell on it. In Portland power was lost, and people huddled around their fireplaces, cooking at the hearth and trying to stay warm. The major streets of Powell, Division, and Stark were impassable, cutting off traffic between Gresham and the city. On the coast hurricane-force winds of 80 miles per hour tore down telephone lines, smashed plateglass windows, and tossed boats from their moorings. Astoria had its worst winter in thirty-two years, with more than a foot of snow. Along the Santiam Highway, between Salem and the Cascades, a 200-foot-long stretch collapsed 12 feet into the ground under the burden of snow.

From throughout the state came reports of blocked highways, severe injuries, and snowbound cities. Klamath Falls was officially closed; the state highway patrol erected roadblocks that prevented anyone from leaving town. Officers had already rescued seven people from the highways surrounding the city, and they were afraid that drivers would become stranded in the huge drifts. Fourteen inches of snow had fallen in eleven hours, and the winds raged at 75 miles per hour.

The citizens of Oakridge, southeast of Eugene, were marooned by dozens of trees that had fallen across the highways. The trees were so laden with ice that they simply laid themselves down. All communication was also cut off, since telephone and power lines were down as well. Six buses filled with passengers were stuck on the highway, as were many other drivers. Even the trains could not get through—a snow-and-rock slide had covered the tracks.

Fifteen miles west of Vernonia, in the mountains near the Oregon coast, sixty people were stranded for three days at the McGregor logging camp. Several attempts were made to reach them before they were rescued. First, a team with a bulldozer tried to reach them from a logging road that approached the camp from the south. But the rescuers went only 2 miles in one day. The trains eventually had better luck—a railroad snowplow inched its way through 15 miles of snowdrifts, finally reaching the camp.

Amazingly, only three people were thought to have died directly from the blizzard. One was a man who had a heart attack while putting chains on his car. Another was a farmer who died when one of his sheds, burdened with snow and ice, collapsed on him. The third was Bonne McNeil. He had lived in a remote cabin near Cave Junction. He was found by some snowshoers on a trail near his house, frozen to death. The group carried Mr. McNeil out on a sled along a 12-mile path created by snowplows.

Meanwhile, at Elk Prairie, 20 miles south of the small town of Molalla, things were looking dire. Elk Prairie is a remote farming region of about 100 square miles encompassing Butte Creek and the headwaters of the Molalla River. Elk Prairie had been cut off from everything for weeks by the deepest snowfall ever recorded in the area. And though it was remote, there were a lot of family farms and livestock that were in danger of starvation. The last mail had been delivered on January 3. The phone lines were gone.

A group of Elk Prairie farmers decided they could no longer wait to be rescued. They were going to have to take matters into their own hands. Among them were Jack Combs, Harold Gibbony, John and Chris Kautz, Gene Katz Jr., and Curtis Thompson, along with four others, and these ten men put together a plan to seek help. First, they tried to visit all the families in the area to see what they needed, reaching about two-thirds of them.

Then, armed by this knowledge, they planned their journey. They would adapt a tractor so that it could go over the snow, attach a sled, and get out to the main road. They knew of a truck that had been left near the Maple Grove school, 10 miles from Elk Prairie. It was on a main road likely to have been plowed. If they could get to the truck, they could haul supplies back on the sled.

The group met at the Sun Dial Ranch and set about modifying the tractor. They bolted wooden planks on the tracks of the tractor. These extended about 2 feet on either side of it and were designed to keep it from sinking into the snow—rather like snowshoes. Setting off from the ranch, the group found the going very slow. Even though the tracks of the trailer were widened, it sank anyway, rather often. The snow was 15 feet deep in some places. To bolster the roadway the men used boards from old buildings, chopped down posts, and otherwise used anything they could find. The first two nights, they made so little progress that they went back to the ranch to sleep, returning the next morning to pick up where they'd left off.

On the third night they reached the Maple Grove school, outside the hamlet of Maple Grove. It was too far to go back, but the tractor had failed yet again. They decided to stay the night in the school. The next morning, Combs, Gibbony, the Kautz brothers, and Gene Katz were back on tractor duty. In the meantime Curtis Thompson put on his snowshoes and hiked the other direction, down to Scotts Mills, 9 miles away. When he arrived, he asked that the local radio station broadcast to the community that the party was safe—and to let someone know that the necessities of daily living were running short in Elk Prairie, maybe there was someone who could do something about it.

The others finally reached Maple Grove on Tuesday afternoon, found the truck, and started out for Molalla. But their trials were not over, for the truck soon skidded into a snowdrift and got stuck there. Finally, they were rescued by a local resident, Charles Novak, who pulled the truck out. At last, by nightfall, the five men reached Molalla, where they spent a weary night. The next day, they loaded the truck with provisions and set back on the difficult return journey to the grateful families in Elk Prairie. There, they waited, like everyone else in Oregon, for an elusive spring that was still months away.

C H A P T E R 8

AN OCTOBER ODDITY

The Columbus Day Storm

1962

The beginning of October is one of the most beautiful times of the year in Oregon. There's a bit of chill in the air in the morning, but the days are still warm. The leaves are noticeably yellow and red, but it's often sunny, and even when it rains, the showers are a welcome respite from the dusty late summer. The rain is not yet relentless.

October storms are, however, part of this package, and there is always some blustery storm to announce the arrival of fall. Yet the Columbus Day Storm of 1962 was different. It was one of those weather events that everyone remembers with great clarity as a defining point in one's personal history.

It arrived on a fair October day. A storm had been predicted, but then, as now, people don't take predictions of dire weather very seriously, especially since this storm was thought to be just an ordinary little autumn blow that might drop some leaves to the ground.

It began far across the Pacific, in the Philippines, as a typhoon named "Freda." During the first week of October, this storm traveled east across the Pacific, gathering energy as it blew. By Columbus Day it was a full-fledged hurricane that was about to bear down mightily on the coast of Oregon.

And bear down it did—the winds at Mount Hebo Air Force Radar Station on the Oregon coast were the highest ever recorded for the state: 170 miles per hour. This initial hit put people inland on the alert, but in Portland it took some frantic calls from Salem, 45 miles to the south, to really drive the message home. At Portland's major newspaper, the *Oregonian,* reporters were on the phone with people in Salem. Their Salem contacts were remarking on what a fierce storm it was turning out to be. They were battening down the hatches. Then suddenly . . . nothing.

In Portland the air was calm. Indeed, it was eerily calm, and many people noticed the stillness and thought it odd. Portland often has an afternoon breeze, but on this day, some say it was still as death. They remember an eerie green light. And the clouds—people remember the clouds, dramatic and beautiful, but unsettling.

About 5 P.M. the winds began to increase.

Houses across the region trembled and shook. People flattened themselves on the floor, moving toward the interiors of their houses, hoping that windows wouldn't shatter, hoping that the walls would stop moving in and out as if they were breathing. Many people remember huddling with their families in lantern light, reading out loud or listening to the radio broadcasting—anything to drown out the sound of the screaming wind. In downtown Portland, where winds reached 116 miles per hour, walls did collapse and windows did shatter—the great plateglass windows in all the storefronts and hotels and restaurants along Broadway and beyond. Giant trees were

An incredible number of trees were uprooted in the Columbus Day storm of 1962—both in cities and in the forests.
PHOTO COURTESY NATIONAL WEATHER SERVICE PORTLAND

uprooted and tossed aside, like weeds in a garden. The shriek and whine of the storm was supernatural and terrifying.

It was over in just a few hours, moving north to Seattle. Residents there said that the wind made the new Space Needle hum like a tuning fork.

But back in Oregon there were stories to tell and a lot of cleaning up to do.

At about 7 P.M. men and women began to emerge from wherever they were keeping themselves safe. The night was strangely silent. There were no lights, and it was quiet except for the sound of broken wires flapping about. The wind had upended so many trees and demolished so many signs and shattered so much glass that the landscape was foreign. It was easy to get lost—not only was it difficult to see where you were and know where you were going, but street after street was blocked with fallen trees and debris. The roof at Multnomah Stadium in southwest Portland (now PGE Park)—which had been filling up with spectators to a football game—had been sheared off by the force of the wind. On the Columbia River three men were endangered when the 18-foot boat they were attempting to protect from the storm broke free of its mooring. The boat, called *The Emancipator,* capsized and threw the men in the water.

Only five of Portland's ten Willamette-spanning bridges were open after the storm. The rest had suffered too much wind damage to be safe. The Hawthorne Bridge was wrecked by a barge that had come unmoored and smashed into it. All through the rivers were boats, houseboats, docks, and other structures, drifting along in the current.

The Oregon coast took the brunt of the storm, suffering the largest hit and the most damage. Town after town reported that every plateglass window of every business was smashed. In Port Orford the high school was obliterated. Downtown buildings collapsed, one nearly killing two women. Gold Beach had had two days of major windstorms, the first one not as severe, but the second turning the town into a mass of debris. Twelve families in this small town had to abandon their homes.

Eugene suffered a great deal of damage, including the destruction of the clock tower atop historic Deady Hall, one of the oldest buildings in Eugene. The tower came crashing down on the lawn. Two Eugene sawmills also burned to the ground. Many ancient, landmark trees were also lost. Nearby, in Junction City, at the height of the storm a fire broke out and, fanned and fed by the wind, engulfed 2 square blocks.

Thirty-eight people died in the storm, and hundreds were injured. Michael Gensel, a two-year-old boy, died when a tree fell on him after he followed his mother outside during the fiercest part of the storm. Such stories were common throughout the state—most people were killed by falling trees, roofs, or debris.

But the wreckage was so severe that it seemed as though many more people must have died—in the days after the storm, rumors were flying that the official count was a lie. For how could people survive such a storm? Part of the explanation lay in the fact that many in Portland had checked into downtown hotels rather than risk a drive home in such a storm. The Benson, the Sheraton, and the Heathman all reported that every room was booked. The hotels were also generous about letting people stay out of harm's way who did not—in fact, who could not, given the capacity of the hotels—book a room. Many refugees from Multnomah Stadium found themselves safely tucked in a hotel bar for the duration of the storm.

The Columbus Day Storm caused long-term damage as well. The estimated cost of the damage was $800 million in today's figures, but it wasn't only the money. In the forests many of Oregon's few remaining 1,000-year-old trees were toppled in the storm, suggesting the rarity and impact of this event. Likewise, in the cities so many old trees were uprooted

Winds reached 116 miles per hour in Portland and 170 miles per hour on the coast. PHOTO COURTESY NATIONAL WEATHER SERVICE PORTLAND

that it became a hallmark of the storm—today, throughout Eugene, Salem, and Portland, when you see a street with long-settled houses, bereft of trees, you'll know that the Columbus Day Storm paid a momentary call.

Throughout western Oregon the storm also ruined many a farmer's crops. Gone were the onion, potato, and corn crop. And the damage to fruit trees—especially the apples and pears, which were still in the middle of their harvest—was incalculable. Barns were flattened, killing livestock. In fact old barns are comparatively rare in western Oregon, since so many of them were blown apart. Eyewitnesses tell of watching roofs peel off the tops of the barn, then being inundated in cyclones of hay.

More than 50,000 houses were damaged or destroyed. After the storm few Oregonians had electricity, and the power would take days to restore. Officials at Portland General Electric sounded dazed. They had never experienced anything like this storm before, where so much damage was done in so little time to so many people. They simply would not predict how long it would take to get everyone back on the grid. They didn't know what was involved. But one clue about the work that lay ahead for them was found in the statements by the regional power authority, the Bonneville Power Administration, which controlled the power from the large dams on the Columbia River. Normally, they processed four million kilowatts per hour. Now they were down to two million. Plus, two of their huge lines were knocked onto the ground, and their dam tower had been blown into the Columbia River.

Disaster always brings profit to some. Business boomed at the city dump, which was charging 25 cents per load to help people get rid of their debris. The county dump also was busy, though they charged twice as much. But you had to choose one or the other, for open burning was strictly forbidden—there were too many open gas and electric lines.

A striking thing about the day after the storm was the glint of glass, everywhere. The sun was shining and people were busily rebuilding and repairing. But everywhere you looked, bits of glass caught the sun. For months little bits of glass swept into corners and crevices served as reminders of the storm.

CHAPTER 9

A COASTAL CATASTROPHE

Tsunami

1964

In January 2005, in response to the great Indian Ocean tsunami the month before, seismologists went before Congress and said that a cataclysmic, tsunami-producing earthquake was pretty likely sometime in the next fifty years. The Cascadia Subduction Zone, the great swath of moving earth beneath the ocean, west of Oregon and Washington, stretching all the way to Alaska, was due for one. And if there were ever an earthquake measuring 9.0 in the Cascadia Subduction Zone, it could take as little as fifteen minutes for a giant wave, perhaps 45 feet high, to engulf the West Coast. It would probably wipe out roads and bridges and thwart any emergency response.

How do they know it could happen? It already has.

On March 27, 1964, Alaska was struck by one of most powerful earthquakes ever recorded, at 8.6 on the Richter scale. The center of this quake was in the Pacific Ocean, and it generated a colossal wave that gathered height as it raced south toward the coasts of Washington, Oregon, and California, where it crashed with great energy. The effects were felt as far away as Louisiana, and dock workers in New Orleans noticed a sudden swell of 6 feet.

Most of the damage occurred in Crescent City, California, where twenty-two people were killed, but Oregon suffered major damage as well. Thousands of people were left without telephone or electrical lines. Houses were destroyed, ships sunk, harbors flooded, bridges thrown down, seawalls breached, and people swept away.

The first wave came roaring in with a sound like thunder, at 11:30 P.M. Surges of anywhere from 3 to 25 feet were reported from towns all along the coast. Seaside suffered through a 10-foot wave, while along the Nehalem River, near Wheeler and Nehalem, the wave reached nearly 12 feet. At Depoe Bay, Newport, Florence, Reedsport, and Brookings, the wave was recorded at 11 feet or higher. At Coos Bay it was 14 feet. Some communities were affected little more than they would have been in an unusually high tide. But many towns experienced significant destruction from the first wave and the three that followed it.

At Cannon Beach a wall of water surged up Elk Creek and took out the bridge. Huge rocks and logs were cast onto lawns all through town. Winchester Bay lost 200 feet of its jetty. Waldport suffered major damage to its waterfront. Two float houses that held local businesses were washed away. One, a lunch counter and tackle store, was swept from its mooring and lost at sea. The other, a restaurant known as The Fisherman's Inn, was smashed to pieces. Along U.S. Highway 101, driftwood thrown onto the highway caused several accidents, and one car was totaled, though the driver wasn't hurt.

Some attempt was made to evacuate on the north coast, but it was not particularly well organized—in part because the tidal wave alarm had been sounded before and had come to nothing. After any earthquake the habit had been to send an advisory to local authorities, who were then supposed to notify residents. But Carl Bondietti, the Clatsop County sheriff, said that this notification arrived a little too late. Human nature being what it is, people didn't take much notice of the routine warning. They had had two false alarms in the months before the tsunami. Bondietti would have needed two hours to evacuate Cannon Beach, and he was alerted only fifteen minutes before the wave hit. "We have yelled wolf before," he said. "I have said some day we were going to find it at the door, and it happened."

Gearhart received its warning on time, and members of the volunteer fire department went from house to house, telling people to evacuate. Most did, leaving town altogether. Ironically, Gearhart was among the least damaged towns on the coast. Other people were warned less officially. One man, Bruce Dymond, was staying with his family in a beachfront cottage at Tolovana Park, just south of Cannon Beach. He got a call from a frantic relative who could see the wave as it approached the shore. He gathered his wife and children and they made a run for their car, reaching it just as the first wave engulfed the cottages. He and his family slept in their car that night, as did a lot of other people who were nervously lining the highways in case they needed to leave in a hurry.

Florence, in the center of coastal Oregon, at the mouth of the Yaquina River, was one of the hardest-hit towns. It was pounded by the series of waves—one of them 16 feet high—that washed over seaside properties, destroying houses, boats, motels, and other property. The water also surged up the Yaquina River, obliterating the riverfront far upriver. In fact the damage all along the coast was greatest in such estuary channels. The collision of the tidal surge with the river flow can amplify the height of the wave, and that is precisely what happened in Florence.

Farther south, in Coos Bay, fishing boats were cast adrift, and two of them sank. At Sunset Beach State Park, near Coos Bay, Leland Stanley was thought to be drowned. He had been walking on the beach before the wave hit, and his wife reported him missing. They were later reunited—luckily, he had escaped harm. But his wife had an even more dramatic escape. She had been sitting in their camper when the wave hit. It picked the truck up and deposited it atop a picnic table.

Some of the worst damage was done to Depoe Bay. The bay contains a seawall that protects the harbor, and the water from the tsunami poured into the bay, roiling the bay and everything in it into a frenzy. The water then broke through the seawall and wreaked havoc on the boats that were moored there. Then it moved on to demolish a 60-foot dock that had been specifically built to withstand high seas.

Witnesses at Gold Beach, on the south coast, observed that the wave didn't look like a normal swell, but rippled independently of the rest of the ocean, in successive pulses. Damage to Gold Beach was increased because the spring salmon season had just opened, and more boats than usual were harbored along the Rogue River.

If the wave had not hit at 11:30 at night, the loss would have been much greater. Hours before, thousands of people had been on the beaches—walking, beachcombing, playing. The early spring weather had been beautiful, drawing people out to the lovely sandy beaches of the Oregon coast. But by 11:30 the beaches were mostly deserted. The next wave, which struck at about 3:00 A.M., also was less damaging than it might have been. By then, the tide was out, and the wave hit farther away from shore. Still, it was powerful enough to breach seawalls up and down the coast, exacerbating the damage from the first wave.

Sheriff Bondietti of Clatsop County was relieved that fewer people hadn't been out on the beautiful starlit night when the wave hit. Given the astonishing death toll from the December 2004 Indian Ocean tsunami, Oregon's death toll from the 1964 wave seems weak. One woman in Seaside died from a heart attack after the wave. Otherwise, only four people died directly from the impact.

But what a sad loss they were! The McKenzie family of Tacoma, Washington, had been sleeping in a driftwood shelter at Beverly Beach State Park. The parents had taken their four children on a camping trip. They were mourning the loss of their eldest child. She had died eight months before—burned to death when, as she was attempting to light a bonfire, her clothes caught on fire.

Mr. McKenzie told the *Oregonian* that the first wave woke the family up and the children began to scream. There were about 12 inches of air at the top of the shelter the family desperately tried to reach. "Logs were thrown at us like match sticks," he told the paper. The receding wave carried the four children—Ricky, Louis, Bobby, and Tammy—out to sea. Ricky's body was recovered the next day, but the fruitless search for the other three continued for days. The parents were treated for lacerations—and shock.

Seismologists predict that when the next tsunami hits, it could be as large as 36 feet. As the 1964 wave shows, some communities will be harder hit than others. After the December 2004 tsunami, coastal communities ran a number of drills to evaluate their readiness for the next one. The results were mixed, showing much work is to be done if residents are to be thoroughly prepared. And even then, human nature being what it is, residents might fail to pay attention.

But maybe not. Visitors to the Oregon coast are often intrigued by the little blue signs that show a universal human figure fleeing a giant wave. These are the signs that indicate the tsunami evacuation route. Seeing them, you know you are in the danger zone. If you hear the tsunami warning siren, you are supposed to follow the signs to higher, safer ground. But that's provided you get the warning on time, that you can see the signs, and that the roads aren't choked with traffic. The signs would not have helped the McKenzies, who lost all their children in the dead of night, swept out to sea in a giant wave.

CHAPTER 10

A WET CHRISTMAS

The Willamette River Flood 1964

That it rains in December in Oregon will not surprise most readers. But several times each century, it rains an amount that surprises even Oregonians, and when that happens, you can be sure that flooding is on the way.

Our winter storms are common from October to May, brought by winds from the west that carry snow to the mountains and rain to the great Willamette Valley, the wide basin that holds most of the people in Oregon. It is some of the richest agricultural land in the world, and when settlers from the eastern part of the United States arrived in the mid-1800s, they thought they had reached the land of milk and honey. It was, but it was also the land of the winter rains.

Oregon's winter weather is determined by two major forces: the polar jet stream and the Pacific Ocean. For the most part the polar jet stream stays to the north, keeping the really cold air in Canada. Each winter, of course, is a little bit different. Every so often, the polar jet stream moves south, bringing with it snow that covers the mountains, foothills, and valleys of western Oregon. Everything closes down as western Oregonians dust off the snowplows and unearth the tire chains. But sometimes this winter reverie is cut short by a warm air current from the southwest. It is nicknamed the "Pineapple Express" because it comes from the Pacific Ocean near Hawaii, and it blows warm air throughout the state, melting the snows even from the highest peaks of the Cascades. It also carries a great deal of rain, intensifying the amount of water in rivers and streams and saturating the valley floor.

The Pineapple Express has been responsible for the worst Willamette River floods in Oregon, including two nearly one hundred years apart, in 1861 and in 1964. In early December 1861, the Willamette River, fed by its overflowing streams and tributaries, flooded to levels not seen before or since. Towns all through the Willamette Valley were washed away. Pioneer diaries record piteous tales of loss: houses, barns, animals, all swallowed by the raging Willamette. The flood covered more than 500,000 acres and rose up to 20 feet above normal in some places. Almost miraculously in view of the rapidity of the flood, the number of deaths was low—twelve persons were known to have perished—but the financial loss was incalculable. It was enough to send many pioneers to drier parts of the West. They crossed back over the Cascades to farm in the arid grasslands of eastern Oregon, or they left for the gold mines of Idaho. The 1861 flood is to this day regarded as the worst flood in recorded history to inundate the valley.

But it has a close rival: the Christmas flood of 1964. It was spawned by heavy snows in mid-December, which brought with them the hope of a white Christmas. These hopes were crushed by the Pineapple Express, which followed the snows with warm, saturating rain—inches and inches of it. Some places received the equivalent of a year's worth of rain in just a few days. Albany's rainfall for December is usually about 7 inches; in 1964 the December total was nearly 13 inches. Detroit, Oregon, received 18 extra inches of rain that month. At Crater Lake, in the Cascades, the normal rainfall for December is about 12 inches. In 1964, it was 38.47.

First it was the snow, and then it was the rain. Then it was the flood. A few days before Christmas, the rivers and streams of western Oregon began to swell. Louise Moody, who lived in the small mountain resort town of Rhododendron, wrote in the *Oregonian* that by December 22, it had been raining steadily on top of the 8 inches of snow that lay on the ground, and the wind had been blowing at 60 miles per hour all around the Mount Hood town. "The ground is soaked with water," she observed, "and can hold no more." She was right—by that morning, the ZigZag Creek, which Rhododendron is built along, was about to overflow its banks and wash away houses and bridges.

Earlier that day, the Oregon State Patrol had evacuated the schoolhouse of the tiny community, escorting the teachers and students across the precarious ZigZag Creek bridge on foot. But people from all across the state were reporting mud slides, closed roads, and silent airports. Reservoirs were engulfed and could not release their water—in fact the Dorena Dam in the western Cascades recorded water 8 feet over its top. By the end of the flood, every river in Oregon was above flood stage, more than thirty major bridges across the state were unusable, thousands of people had been evacuated, and seventeen people had died.

Rural towns took the brunt of the disaster. The communities in the Mount Hood area were especially hard hit. Bridges were the first to go, and then the houses, more than one hundred of them washed into the creeks and rivers that nestled on the mountain and its foothills. They lost all their power, and no one could reach them save by helicopter, since bridges and roads were impassable. The story of the hamlet of Wildcat Creek, near Rhododendron, is representative. This tiny rural community lay at the bottom of a hill east of the town of Sandy, just west of Mount Hood. The hillsides around it had been had been logged off, which destabilized the land, and the normally serene creek was a raging torrent—perfect conditions to create the avalanche that wiped out the town. Giant logs, mud, rocks, and debris tumbled down the hillside, destroying fifteen houses. Making things worse was the fact that the flooding Wildcat Creek blew out the road, tearing 20-foot wide holes in the roadbed. This situation totally isolated the town, for up the road, the Rhododendron bridge had also been wiped out.

One elderly couple at Wildcat Creek, Mr. and Mrs. Harry Engle, lost their home and more. Their house was a direct target of the avalanche. Mr. Engle's neighbor, Mrs. Robert Vallereux, told the *Oregonian* that she was speaking with him on the telephone when she heard a terrifying sound, like an approaching train. Running to the door, she looked out to see Harry Engle in his own doorway. "Suddenly," she said, "there came a roar, and logs and dirt and rocks came rushing by, crashing into his home, and I didn't see him anymore." But Mrs. Engle was trapped in the house. Her neighbors Thomas Day and Carl Neumann daringly rescued her—they had to rig up emergency lines and anchor them tightly, then wade 20 feet across the swift, deep creek. They could not find Mr. Engle, who had been buried in the avalanche.

Avalanches were not the only danger. From all over the state, came woeful tales of drownings and electrocutions. Gary

First, a twelve-year-old boy from Millington, near Coos Bay, reached for a lamp in his darkened, flooded house. But the lamp's wires were live and he died from an electrical shock he received as his hand brushed the surface of the lamp. In Gresham a man named Harry Stroh also died from shock as he repaired power lines on his property. In John Day, Dr. Robert Dickson was traveling across the John Day Dam Bridge when it was destroyed, washed away by flooding. Others drowned when their cars skidded off the road, while they were fleeing rising waters, or while attempting to rescue their belongings.

In Yamhill County, southwest of Portland, the damage was severe. Many of the small towns were isolated by the rising water. The bridge between Newberg and St. Paul had to be closed. Its wooden pillars were under severe strain from the mighty flood of the Willamette. The road between Newberg and Wilsonville was also blocked off, trapping hundreds. Those who lived along the banks of the river sought refuge in churches and schools in the Yamhill County towns of Sheridan and Willamina. The sheriff complained that the Columbus Day Storm, which was just two years prior, was nothing compared with this Christmas Day flood. At least the Columbus Day Storm was over quickly.

Coastal towns pay a high price for their beautiful settings, and this flood was part of that reckoning. The Oregon coast suffered extreme damage. In Reedsport the business district was flooded with 8 feet of water. Rescue crews also had to evacuate dozens of people who were staying at Reedsport's resorts for the holidays. A little farther south, in Coos Bay, a colossal log and debris jam contributed to the flooding that swamped more than thirty houses. It took three large tugboats several days to loosen the jam. Still farther down the coast, in Curry

County, both Brookings and Gold Beach took a beating. Their ports were obliterated by the flood. At Gold Beach the dike and boat-turning basin, painstakingly rebuilt after the Columbus Day Storm, were both gone, along with 250 fishing and recreation boats. A similar story was heard in Brookings, which had been the victim of a massive wall of debris that had bulldozed down the Chetco River and right through the boat-basin wall.

Back in the center of the state, the Willamette had been transformed from a serene and utilitarian conduit to a roiling terror. Oregon City stood in many feet of water. In fact the churning waterfalls that normally characterize the Willamette there had completely disappeared under the sheet of water that flooded the city. Downriver in Portland, the lower deck of the Steel Bridge not only was underwater, but had also been hit by a 1,000-piece log raft. This mass of wood had broken from a larger log boom near Oregon City and sped off downstream, slamming into all the river bridges as it went. It damaged the Hawthorne Bridge, in the center of Portland, so much that it was closed for a year.

In Portland the Willamette reached 29.8 feet—12 feet above flood stage. Since 1861, only the Vanport Flood in 1948 had seen a higher reading. The force of the flood hit at noon on Christmas Day. Workers had spent the few days between the worst part of the storm and the ensuing flood shoring up the flood walls that line the banks of the Willamette as it coursed through the city. Three-foot-high walls made from concrete and sandbags barely held back the water. The river carried a mass of debris with it, and where the city was unprotected by dikes, the water and debris wrought destruction. The railroad tracks at Union Station lay beneath a foot of water.

Portland has two rivers to contend with—not only the Willamette, but also the Columbia. This flood set a new record for water flow in the latter river. No one could recall both rivers having such high waters ever before. In North Portland the fears of the Vanport flood of 1948 were resurrected when 1,200 houses between the Columbia River, Columbia Boulevard, and Northeast 33rd Avenue had to be evacuated—and there were so many spectators watching the evacuation that the sheriff had to close the bridge that spans the Columbia between Vancouver and Portland. The city was afraid that, as they did during the 1948 flood, the railroad dikes would give way and swamp the city. The Multnomah County sheriff was told by the Army Corps of Engineers that water was seeping through the massive dikes and that they might give way. And the water was lapping near the top of the dike, less than 2 feet from the top of the tracks.

After the 1861 flood some people left the area. But most people stayed and rebuilt their farms and houses. Over the years more people came, and Willamette was rerouted, rechanneled, and dammed. By the 1940s it was a very different river. Dams regulated the flow of the water, and it stayed in a central channel, so that even at times of flooding, the water would not cover the entire valley. The U.S. Army Corps of Engineers has estimated that the 1964 flood would have reached even higher levels if not for the regulation of the water—perhaps as much as 10 feet higher.

Nonetheless, the flood managed to do hundreds of millions of dollars worth of damage, as well as incalculable loss to the well-being of thousands of Oregonians. The flood seemed especially brutal because of its timing, arriving at Christmas and preceded by a storm that caused plenty of damage on its own. Thousands were homeless; many lost everything. But many were just grateful to survive. From all over the state came stories that made the timing of the storm especially poignant. Six truckers left their trucks and walked home across the Siskiyou Mountains to be with their families for Christmas. Other people had to stay where they were. About fifty travelers were stuck at a roadside truck stop near the Biggs junction along the Columbia River in eastern Oregon. And stranded they were—several were even evicted from their motel rooms on Christmas Day. People were running out of money, and there was little Christmas cheer. Because all the east-west highways in the state were closed—each and every one—no one could get back to Portland.

One of these people was a truck driver who worked for Robert Nelson Bates, owner of the Bates Trucking Company in Portland. When this driver told Mr. Bates about all the people stranded in Biggs, Bates suggested that the driver distribute the thirty turkeys he was supposed to be delivering to Portland. Elsewhere, across the region, offers of help, food, clothing, and money poured in. Those with access to small planes and helicopters brought food and water to the numerous small towns that had been cut off by the floods. These many kindnesses were received with gratitude. Indeed, Louise Moody reported that one boy in Rhododendron was able to really put things in perspective after this outpouring of generosity. "We don't need a bridge very bad," he said, "because they can bring in Santa Claus in one of the helicopters."

CHAPTER 11

MAYDAY IN AUGUST

The Brookings-Harbor Rescues

1972

Early morning drizzle misted Brookings, Oregon—nothing out of the ordinary, even in mid-August, even in Brookings, which was usually warmer than the rest of the coast. It certainly didn't stop the fishermen who were gearing up for the day, drinking coffee and eating breakfast. The seas looked calm; the Coast Guard hadn't raised any storm flags; the National Weather Service in Portland predicted mild winds of 10 to 20 knots, some showers, and partial clearing later in the day. The day before had brought reports of excellent fishing offshore, near Point St. George, a little more than 15 miles to the south, just past the California border. August 16, 1972, looked like it would be a good day for fishing, too.

But not everyone was sure. One fisherman had been out without much luck for three days, north of Brookings and to the west of Gold Beach. His name was Bill, and his boat was the *Manatee*. Bill was a little spooked. He couldn't see any birds—usually there were a lot of them, following the schools of fish that traveled close to shore. Maybe the birds weren't having any luck either.

The south coast of Oregon is a wild and lonely place, then and now. In 1972 the Brookings area was home to several thousand people who made their living from trees and tourists and fish, people who knew well how volatile the sea can be. Brookings and its small neighboring hamlet, Harbor, lie along the coast where the Chetco River empties into the Pacific Ocean, about 4 miles north of the California-Oregon border. To the east are the Siskiyou Mountains and the redwood forests. To the south, toward California, the land slopes into low cliffs. To the north the beautiful sandy beaches are guarded by windswept, monolithic rocks. Small craft and large are warned to stay clear of the coast, since the rocks and reefs are treacherous.

The evening before, on August 15, the Coast Guard reported the weather as good, with northerly winds at less than 10 knots. In fact the only unusual report was an "ominous calm" prevailing just north of the Point St. George reef. The next morning, however, the weather conditions suddenly changed. At 5:30 A.M. fishing boats in the Cape Mendocino and Humboldt Bay areas, about 100 miles south of the Chetco River, were reporting southerly storm winds of up to 60 knots, and reports of these winds moved steadily northward throughout the early morning hours of August 16. At 5:58 A.M. the Humboldt Bay Coast Guard Station received word that a small but severe storm was gathering. They were asked to tell the Coast Guard in Crescent City and recommended that no boats be allowed to leave the harbor. No one thought to tell the Chetco River station, far to the north, in an entirely different Coast Guard district.

So there were no ominous red-and-black storm flags waving at the Chetco River station that morning, and the Brookings-

Harbor fishing fleet went about its business as usual. The *Karen I* left at 5 A.M. The *Donna N* left at 6. The *Dixie Lee* left the harbor right before dawn, at 5:45, with Clayton Dooley as captain. His grandson David Shinkle was helping out that day. They didn't see anything worrisome in the weather, noting in the log a 6-knot southeasterly wind and slightly choppy conditions. The *Dixie Lee* was sturdy and seaworthy, and Clayton Dooley had been a commercial fisherman for years.

Writer Jayne Gibney was also awake early that morning. Her husband was fishing 100 miles north, off Coos Bay, with the tuna fleet. She turned up the volume on her CB radio. The CB radio was the favored means of communication among the fishermen and their families. It was convenient, and, unlike bulky ship-to-shore radios, it fit on board even the smallest boats. The Coast Guard wanted everyone to use the ship-to-shore radio, especially when boats were in distress, since the Coast Guard wouldn't be able to hear Mayday calls broadcast on CB—they didn't have access to CB radio. Government agencies were forbidden from using them: CB radio was designated for the people, rather than the government or the military, so the Coast Guard couldn't use it to monitor unfolding events. But people preferred CB—it was simple to use, and effective. Gibney, like many fishermen's wives, had it on whenever she was awake, and it provided the soundscape to her day.

Gibney also followed the weather closely. She looked at her barometer. It was falling—in fact the bottom had dropped out. But the weather reports on the local radio station made no mention of any storm or even any bad weather. The radio station got its information from the National Weather Service post in Portland, hundreds of miles away, but the local fishermen relied on it.

One fisherman was not out that morning—Jim Carson from the *Mabel Jean*. That morning, he was at home monitoring his ship-to-shore radio, and what he heard wasn't good. About 7 A.M. he sent out a warning on CB channel 8 that winds were fast building from the south. Jim had heard that a tuna boat offshore and to the south had taken 80-mile-per-hour winds. Jayne Gibney heard him and she was not surprised. She had noted her barometer with alarm, since usually the barometer didn't fall quite so fast unless a bad storm was brewing. Someone replied to Jim—a fish processor—who reported that he'd heard from Crescent City, and the boats down there were getting winds of 86 mph. Gibney recalled that "our little boats debated on the weather but as a whole ignored those reports. . . . I knew Jim was absolutely right. He was trying to warn the fishermen who were not as experienced."

Still, the skippers Jim was trying to alert were calm. "So far, no wind. We're not very far out anyway," they said. "We'll be in quick if it starts to blow."

On the Pacific Coast weather can turn quickly and terrible storms can brew in just a few hours. At 9:10, between the Klamath River, south of Crescent City, and Point St. George, the wind abruptly shifted. Five minutes later, strong winds were suddenly gusting on St. George's Reef.

Jayne Gibney, at her CB, heard Bill on the *Manatee*. He was asking for Butch Crook on the *Donna N.* Butch had left his moorage about 6 A.M., accompanied by his son John, who was ten, and his nephew Joel, who was seventeen. The two boys loved to go out with Butch and had been looking forward to this day. Butch and the boys were fishing alongside his friend Gerald Hahn on the *Sea Breeze*. Bill and Butch discussed their fishing, and Bill asked Butch to tell his wife that he would need a ride home when he returned to harbor. Then they discussed the weather. Butch said they had some light breeze from the south, but that the barometer was dropping and that maybe a strong southerly wind was on its way. Bill thought this was strange. He told Butch that the winds where he was, off Gold Beach, were northerly—as well as strong and accompanied by rain. He noted that the winds where he was should also have been from the south.

Clayton Dooley and David Shinkle, aboard the 33-foot *Dixie Lee,* had been trolling since after 7 A.M. about 4 miles from the St. George Reef lighthouse. A little past 9 A.M., they heard Jim from the *Mabel Jean.* A bad storm was definitely on its way. They pulled in their gear and began to head for home.

As the *Dixie Lee* headed back to the Chetco River, the two men managed the stormy seas and gusting winds without any trouble. Dooley was a long-time commercial fisherman, and his nephew was also an experienced sailor. But then the chain holding the *Dixie Lee*'s starboard outrigger snapped. The *Dixie Lee* careened toward port and began to list, caught in a trough. They lost control over the boat, and the waves began pouring into the hatch.

The *Karen I* had departed harbor that morning skippered by William Friend and his wife Virginia Mae. On board were also their two sons, William and Brian, and their neighbor Donald Higgins. They had planned to spend the day salmon fishing. At 8 A.M. another captain, Phillip Evanow of the *Tau Tog,* spotted the *Karen I* and hailed them. The reports of bad weather were now established, and indeed it was obvious that the wind was rising—white caps were starting to form, and the wind was picking up. Evanow thought the *Karen I* seemed to be having some trouble. He advised them to start heading in and even offered to take one of the boys, Mrs. Friend, and Mr. Higgins aboard the *Tau Tog*. But they didn't want to leave their boat.

Most of the sixty-nine boats that put out to sea from Crescent City and Brookings on August 16 were small craft—32 feet or less. For small boats wind is dangerous. A gust of 34 knots—about 40 miles per hour—can easily capsize a small boat; a large wave can knock off an outboard or ruin a rudder; it can leave the skipper powerless before the current, with no way to fight back against the sea. During major storms small craft are barred from leaving the harbor by the Coast Guard. But if a storm arises when they are already out of the harbor, they will have to survive as best they can.

By 9.30 A.M. the first Maydays were coming in, from the Crescent City area. By 10:30 the winds were gusting to 75 knots in the Brookings area. The Mayday calls were coming through both the CB channels and the Coast Guard's ship-to-shore channels. Somehow, the CB channel Maydays had to be relayed to the Coast Guard. At the Coast Guard station, there was only one person on duty, and he had to handle all incoming phone calls as well as the radio. That's because the rest of his crew were on the single boat assigned to the area, the *Cape Carter,* which was already out by Point St. George Reef busy rescuing the *Alegria,* with four passengers aboard.

In Brookings, Jayne Gibney was listening on her CB as the distress calls began pouring in. She helped direct the radio traffic. Her friend Peggy drove down to the harbor and parked outside the Coast Guard station. Peggy's truck had a CB radio in it, and as Jayne heard distress calls, she would relay them to Peggy, who would run into the Coast Guard station and tell the radio monitor. Peggy also told those on shore where help was needed, organizing rescue parties when two boats, the *Christa* and the *D Ann D,* crashed into the beach. She and Jayne directed others with radio units to the breakwaters, where they could also help organize search parties and lifelines. Other volunteers—among them the worried wives of Coast Guard officers and fishermen—made coffee, brought down blankets and towels, and provided other supplies for the rescue efforts.

Out at sea those aboard the small boats were fighting for their lives. The wind was so fierce that the rain drove at them horizontally. Gibney reported that they could not see the shore or one another, and they definitely could not progress against such strong winds. As she recalled it:

> All three channels on the CB radio were filled with Mayday calls. Channel 9, the normal distress channel for the CBs, also was carrying calls from boats in danger, but not nearly as many as on the regular channels that the boats used. The people on the boats simply did not even have the time to switch to the distress channel. Some of the boats were sinking. Some simply called for help and nothing more was heard from them. The seas were building so fast that no one on the boats could tell where they were or see vessels that were actually right beside them.

About 9:40 the *Karen I* put out its first distress call. Donald Higgins, the Friends' neighbor, called for help, and a few minutes later, Friend got on the CB himself, stating he was just a few miles west of the Chetco River whistle buoy. He told the network that his gear was out and that his engine was dead. A while later, Gibney and Boyd Mabry of the *Ocean King*—as well as everyone else on the network—heard a Mayday call from

Virginia Friend. They were dead in the water about a mile and a half from a local rock landmark known as the Stack. Mabry started after them but could not spot the *Karen I*. He radioed them, and they reported they were about 5 miles west of Goat Island, but he still could not find them. About 10:45 Virginia Friend sent out another Mayday, begging for help. They were going down. Everyone on the CB radio heard it, but they could only stand helplessly by, sickened.

The Coast Guard recovered the bodies of Virginia Friend and one of her sons later that afternoon, but the other three aboard the *Karen I* were lost at sea.

When Butch Crook first heard Jim Carson from the *Mabel Jean* warning about the weather and suggesting that small boats should leave, he and Hahn aboard the *Sea Breeze* decided to return to harbor. Within fifteen minutes they were on their way. Butch told Hahn that it was starting to really blow and that they'd have to stay in the trough all the way to shore. This was the last that Hahn heard from the *Donna N*. But back on shore Jayne Gibney heard him one more time. Gibney's friend Jill had come by to help out. They listened together on the CB and over the din of cries and screams, they heard their good friend Butch's voice.

"I can't keep up with it. I'm sinking!"

About the same time Clayton Dooley and David Shinkle were struggling with the *Dixie Lee*. It foundered about 10:30. Just before the boat sank, Dooley and Shinkle put on their life-saving gear and attempted to head for shore. They were not far from the Chetco River buoy, but the seas were high and the wind still roaring, and they had no way to let anyone know where they were. Shinkle helped Dooley as much as he could, trying to keep him alert in the chilly waters. About 1 P.M., however, Shinkle realized his grandfather had died. He stayed by his grandfather, hoping someone would find them. Finally, a boat called the *Pam Bay* picked him up north of Brookings near Goat Island, which is about 500 yards offshore. The *Pam Bay* wasn't able to get Dooley's body aboard, but shortly after the *Pam Bay* rescued Shinkle, a Coast Guard vessel was able to retrieve his grandfather.

Several boats from the Crescent City area also foundered in the storm north of Point St. George. One of these belonged to Joseph Leoni. He fished alone and had no radio, and his body was recovered several days after the storm. Another, the *Mindy Lynn,* an 18-foot fiberglass boat owned by Robert Wilson, left Crescent City at about 6:15 to fish along the Point St. George Reef. Wilson didn't have a radio with broadcast and receiving capacity, though he did have a CB. He sent out a distress call that was answered by Marlon Tolman on the *Carmoreng*. Tolman had some difficulty locating Wilson, and when he did find him, the wind was "whipping [the *Mindy Lynn*] across the seas like a piece of paper." Just as the *Carmoreng* reached the boat—they were only 10 feet apart—its rudder broke off. Now Tolman needed help too. The two men stayed in radio contact as the boats helplessly drifted away from each other. Wilson said he would try to get to Brookings. In the last radio transmission from Wilson, he told Tolman, "My boat has a lot of water in it, I am trying to bail and I don't think I can make it."

The *Bounding Main* radioed for help about 9 A.M. Onboard the 25-foot wooden boat were Dennis Main and his son Matthew. Carl Brower heard the call—like others, Main said he was going to try for Brookings. He was about 7 miles northwest of the St. George Reef Light. About half an hour later, Main radioed Irvin Feyerisen. Feyerisen's boat, the *D Ann D,* was the same make as the *Bounding Main,* and Feyerisen told Main to take it easy, to "wash along with it." But apparently the seas were too rough for the boat and it capsized, for Matthew was lost at sea, and Dennis Main was found the next day, dead from exposure.

Feyerisen, on board the *D Ann D,* had tried to head into the beach but had trouble crossing the bar. He and his wife struggled for hours, and finally at about 3 P.M., Feyerisen made up his mind to wait out the surf near the Chetco buoy. He disengaged the boat's shaft for a moment to slow down as he reached the buoy. But when he tried to put the boat in gear again, he stalled the engine. Investigating, Feyerisen found that his anchor line had washed over the side and become entangled with part of the engine. The only way to fix it was to raise the engine drive unit. Just as he was completing this repair, a wave washed over the *D Ann D,* flooding the motor with seawater and rendering it inoperable. Now the boat had no power. It was drifting toward shore, heading for the breakers, with nothing to stop it. Just as it reached the breaker line, it capsized in the frothy waves. Feyerisen was caught up in the rigging. His wife was thrown onto the shore. She was rescued, however, by a Coast Guard swimmer, Tommy Beadle, who was attached by a lifeline to Chetco River Coast Guard rescuers on the beach. They had spotted the Feyerisens struggling in the surf. Beadle grabbed Mrs. Feyerisen before she was carried back out to sea. Then he and the rest of the rescue swimmers set about detaching her husband from the rigging of the *D Ann D.*

Coast Guard rescuers also saved the life of the skipper of the *Christa.* The *Christa* was the largest boat caught up in the storm; it was a 44-foot fishing boat, and it was foundering on the rocks on the north jetty of Brookings. The *Christa* was breaking apart.

With great skill Coast Guard officer McMichael, the officer in charge, was able to jockey his surfboat to the deep water beyond the breakers, with the fisherman safely on board.

During the storm Brookings was more isolated than ever. The Coast Guard in California wasn't able to communicate with the Coast Guard in Oregon. The boats in distress didn't have time to tell the Coast Guard of their plight. The National Weather Service in Portland received storm warnings only after 11 A.M., well into the storm. And just before 10 A.M., a tree downed the power lines to the only radio station in the area, preventing it from broadcasting. Electricity all over town was cut.

But the amount of traffic on the CB—and its nature—drew attention to this remote corner of the world. Yet even those in Brookings were not aware of the full extent of the disaster while it was happening. Right at the peak of the storm, Jayne Gibney's telephone rang. There were piteous Mayday calls coming over the CB radio, so when she picked up the receiver, she was surprised to find that it was a TV station from Medford, on the other side of the Siskiyou Mountains. They were wondering what was going in Brookings—no one could reach anybody, not the Coast Guard, not the police, not the radio station. What was happening?

Gibney told them a sudden storm had blown in and that a lot of boats were in trouble. People were missing. The reporter seemed to want to keep her on the line—unbeknownst to Gibney, the call was being broadcast live. But Gibney hung up on them. "I have to go," she said. "People are dying here. They need my help."

Nowadays, it's easy to see exactly what the weather is, has been, and will shortly be, just by typing in a zip code on the computer or turning on the television. We take it for granted. We have satellites and the Internet and Doppler radar. The biggest difference between then and now, however, is the proliferation of ways to talk to one another about the weather. Many tools for monitoring it were available then, but there were fewer means of communicating the information.

And in 1971, the year before the storm, the Brookings area had lost one of the few available means of communication. The Coast Guard had decided to replace a ship it had stationed west of Mendocino, California, with a large buoy. The National Weather Service had also used the ship, to collect weather information. The buoy had no way to collect this weather information, however, and thus the National Weather Service no longer had the means to gather early information about local storms. Even worse, the different Coast Guard districts had no way to share information. They did not share teletype circuitry that would have allowed them to simultaneously observe the progress of impending storms. Though reports of the brewing storm were available farther south, no one told the Coast Guard station in Brookings. In fact the weather chart used by the National Weather Service did not even show the storm.

Many on that day were heroic, risking their own lives—for example, Marlon Tolman on the *Carmoreng,* who tried to help Robert Wilson and ended up foundering himself, or those who sought the *Karen I,* or David Shinkle trying to keep his grandfather conscious. The Coast Guard rescued more than forty people and at least fifteen vessels. Some of these people were returned to port by the Coast Guard themselves, while others were able to return under their own power. The Coast Guard's own record keeping was overwhelmed by the sheer volume of distress calls all at once, so they were not even sure exactly how many people they helped. The Coast Guard surf swimmers and sailors—especially Tommy Beadle, Carl Eckard, and Capt. Donald McMichael, who were officially recognized for their bravery and competence—fearlessly met the foundering boats, plucked stranded fishermen from the water, and maneuvered their own craft in dangerous surf and high seas. The official reports of the accident, however, also note that without the assistance of the citizens in Brookings and Crescent City who took their own craft to sea, the loss of life would have been much worse.

One of these citizens was Jim, of the *Mabel Jean*. He had been the first person to warn about the impending storm. When he heard the distress calls, he took the 50-foot *Mabel Jean* out of the harbor. He helped many smaller boats cross the bar and get safely to the harbor—the wind was so fierce that the waves were breaking across the bar, rather than on the shore. As a result smaller boats could not cross the bar without capsizing or being thrown against the rocky jetties, and many skiffs were found upside down. So Jim turned the *Mabel Jean* sideways, blocking the wind and creating the space for smaller boats to get safely between the jetties. He saved many this way. Then, after the storm had blown through, he put to sea to search for survivors, in particular for Butch Crook and the boys, and the Friend family, searching until dark.

The Coast Guard reported that little will ever be known about most of the boats were lost that day. They knew that the *Dixie Lee* had a broken outrigger and that this led to the boat listing and foundering in the large swells. That's what they believe happened to the *Karen I*—likely, it was swamped or broken up by the seas after it lost power. But the loss of the *Donna N* remains a mystery. The Coast Guard reported that "the vessels involved simply could not cope with existing weather conditions and other contributing factors such as a broken outrigger and loss of propulsion power."

Today, the Brookings-Harbor Marina is a pretty, working harbor, with fishing boats busily putting out to sea and returning with their catch, as well as a thriving tourist attraction. There are gift shops and restaurants, fishing docks and park benches. In a quite corner, though, is the Mariners Memorial, a monument to the thirteen people who died at sea that day. It was rededicated on August 15, 1999, twenty-five years after the storm, to ensure that we would remember what happened.

The memorial will keep the story alive. But those who witnessed the storm require no memorial, for they are haunted by the voices of those who died that day. As Jayne Gibney in her memoir, *There Were No Birds,* writes: "Although nearly all of the men and women at sea during the hours of violent wind stayed reasonably calm, some did not. The sound of crying, pleas for help, and screams coming over the radio that day was something that I would remember all the rest of my life."

CHAPTER 12

"WE'RE GOING DOWN"

The Last Journey of Flight 173

1978

Debra Alloway's phone rang. It was her neighbor, Mr. Buttons. He asked her if she and her family—two baby girls and her husband Allen—were all right. In view of the air crash.

"Air crash?" she said. "What air crash?"

"The plane that went down right at your house! You should go out and look."

As Debra Alloway told the *Oregonian,* she had just moved a few days before, keeping her phone number, but she thanked Mr. Buttons and turned on the television. What she saw shocked her: Where her old house had been, in East Portland between Burnside and 157th Avenue, was nothing but blue smoke and debris. A DC-8 had flattened it. It was United Flight 173, en route from Denver to Portland, and it fell from the sky at 6:14 P.M. on December 28, 1978.

Late December is a busy time to travel, so it was no surprise that Flight 173 was full, with 175 adult passengers, 6 infants, and 8 crew members. People were coming home from their holiday visits, getting ready for the new year. The flight was uneventful for two-and-a-half hours. It was due to arrive a little after 5 P.M., and the pilots had the city in sight.

At 5:05 Capt. Melburn McBroom advised Portland International Airport—PDX in airport code—that the flight was approaching and received clearance to descend. But when Flight 173 lowered its landing gear, Captain McBroom later told NTSB investigators, "It was noticeably unusual and I felt it seemed to go down more rapidly. As my recollection, it was a thump, thump in sound and feel." He was also watching for the gear door light, indicating the landing gear door was open.

"The thump was much out of the ordinary for this airplane. It was noticeably different, and we got the nose gear green light but no other lights," McBroom remembered. He was worried whether the landing gear had actually been let down, or if the thump and the missing light were signs of a big problem—especially since the first officer remarked that the plane seemed to yaw to the right. The flight attendants and passengers had heard the thump, too. Passenger Charles Linderman observed that a "tremendous shudder went through the aircraft as the landing gear was lowered."

Malfunctioning landing gear is an almost certain route to death and disaster. The captain notified PDX, who told him to go ahead and orbit until he got the landing gear problem figured out. So for the next twenty-three minutes, the flight crew reviewed the emergency and precautionary things they were supposed to and could do. They followed the usual procedures, and then they took the extra step of radioing the United Airlines Maintenance Control, in San Francisco. Together, the flight crew and United Maintenance reviewed everything once more. Captain McBroom told them, at 5:40, that he planned to

For a doomed plane, Flight 173 was lucky. PHOTO COURTESY BOB GARRARD

hold on for another fifteen or twenty minutes and said that he had 7,000 pounds of fuel—which should have given him just enough fuel to land.

At 5:44 United Maintenance asked, "You're landing at 5 [minutes] past the hour?"

The captain replied that they were, and that they were preparing the passengers for an emergency landing. But at the same time, they were also preoccupied with the landing gear.

At 5:49 the flight crew noted they had 5,000 pounds of fuel and that the fuel indicators were starting to blink. They were 13 miles southwest of PDX.

But the airport had them change their approach vector, so that they'd come in at a different angle. This meant a longer flying time, and more time to make sure the landing gear was okay, but it also meant they were taking a risk with the fuel.

Captain McBroom told his flight engineer to figure on another fifteen minutes.

Second Officer Mendenhall, the flight engineer, said, "That's gonna run us really low on fuel here."

At 5:51 McBroom told Mendenhall to alert United at PDX—they'd be landing with about 4,000 pounds of fuel in an emergency situation at about 6:05. For the next few minutes, the crew discussed a number of things with one another. They told PDX how much fuel they had. They talked about the passengers—how many there were and whether they were scared. They covered the emergency landing procedures. The airplane was beginning to circle around to the northeast, still south of the city.

At 5:55 the flight engineer reported that the descent check was complete. They were ready to land. A minute later, First Officer Beebe wanted to know how much fuel they had. The flight engineer said 3,000 pounds, and then he went into the cabin to see how things were going. The captain and first officer wanted to make sure the flight attendants had ample time for preparing until their landing; and they also wanted to cover how to evacuate the cockpit.

All the while, they had maintained radio contact with Portland. At 6:05, the crew told PDX they were coming in. At 6:06, the flight engineer returned to the cockpit. He said the passengers were ready and well prepared by the flight attendants—they were all reseated and ready to go, able-bodied men were by the exit doors, and they were all set. A second later, the first officer said, "We're losing the number 4 engine."

"Why?" asked the captain.

"Fuel," said Beebe.

At 6:07, Flight 173 asked for clearance to land immediately. They told PDX that they'd lost two engines. Maybe they could make the Troutdale Airport, a small strip usually occupied by private planes, just east of Portland.

Then Captain McBroom said, "They're all going. We can't make Troutdale."

First Officer Beebe said, "We can't make anything."

At 6:13 Captain McBroom radioed Portland International Airport: "Mayday Portland tower! United 173, heavy, Mayday. We're going down. We're not going to be able to make the airport."

In the cabin the flight attendants told the passengers to put their heads down and grab their ankles. They had already distributed cushions to help break any falls. Then everything went silent.

"We were coming in and there was a thump," recalled passenger Phyllis McLaughlin. "The lights went out and the engines too. There wasn't a sound, only the wind rushing over the wings of the plane. We were gliding."

Then—a rough landing—they bounced a couple of times. They hit the ground, dragging trees and wires, slowing them down. Then they stopped.

United Flight 173, with 189 souls aboard, crashed into a wooded neighborhood full of people in East Portland at 6:14 P.M. It was 6 miles east of the airport. The path of wreckage stretched for 1,554 feet and was 130 feet wide. Eight passengers, plus the flight engineer, Forrest Mendenhall, and the senior flight attendant, Joan Wheeler, were killed. Twenty-one passengers and two crew members were injured seriously.

But—astonishingly—most people walked away.

Inside the cabin passengers were scared. Steven Heitzel, who was returning to his home in Milwaukie, Oregon, said the pilot told them he hoped to touch down normally. But then,

"Boom, boom. . . . I didn't know if we were dead or alive after the crash." The right front part of the airplane was destroyed in the landing; most of the seriously injured passengers were in this part of the cabin, as well as all of those who died. The passengers seated near the wings were also injured, and some were injured during the evacuation, when they had to jump from the exit, or when they climbed through debris on the ground.

For some leaving the plane was a challenge. When they tried to open the exit doors, they were blocked by trees, and the first doors seemed to take about five minutes to open. However, for many it went just as it was supposed to. As one passenger told the *Oregonian:*

> There was some panic when the plane stopped moving. But a boy at the rear of the compartment calmed everybody down. Then the door opened and I jumped out. Somebody caught me. As soon as we were on the ground, everybody started screaming, "Get away from the plane, get away from the plane." They were afraid it was going to explode.

The plane didn't explode, but it did make a horrific sound when it crashed. Linda Byre was at home in Portland when she heard a noise and noticed her lights blink. She looked outside and was shocked by what she saw. She screamed, "It's a plane—a big plane! Call someone! Call anyone!" Another woman reported a loud scraping crash. Then the air filled with a dusty blue fog and out of the dust walked a young man with "white stuff all over him."

Her neighbor, Teresa Salisbury, had been eating dinner with her two-year-old daughter in her Portland home when she heard a loud, frightening sound. The windows shook and rattled and the door flew open. "So I grabbed my kid and went to the back of the house," she said, but saw nothing. Then she went to the front of the house. "And there was all this blue smoke. It was choking me. It was like gas smoke. Then everybody started coming out of the plane." The house next door to hers was totally flattened. But she did help the dazed passengers wandering about. "Five people came to my house to get water, and asked 'Where are we?'"

In fact all the neighbors were having the same conversation. They had all heard the crash. And then they went outside to find scores of frightened people wandering uncertainly. JoAnn Walmer's house was about 200 feet west of the crash site. About twenty-five people came into her house after the landing. Some were lying on the rug in various states of injury—some had broken ribs, some had cuts, some were in shock.

Within moments the scene was swarming with 300 firefighters, paramedics, and police. Area hospitals were put on alert to treat the injured. Medical emergency workers found Capt. Melburn McBroom wandering around the aircraft until they made him sit down so they could treat his injuries.

In a great turn of good luck, no one on the ground was hurt. The crash destroyed two small rental houses, but no one was living in either one on December 28, 1978. One family had moved away about two weeks before. Of those on the ground, perhaps none was more grateful than Debra Alloway. Just twelve days before, she and her family had been evicted from one of the houses that the plane hit. She said she was going to call up the owner of the loan company and thank him for evicting them. "God was up there," she said, "protecting us when he fixed it so we had to move out of there. We're Christians and we read the Bible here at home."

Apparently, someone was also protecting those who didn't read the Bible quite so often, such as Kim Campbell. He was a twenty-seven-year-old convict who was being returned to the Oregon State Penitentiary in Salem to serve concurrent sentences for robbery. Campbell was being returned there because he had already escaped once, from a state penitentiary forest camp in the Oregon Coast Range. He walked away from it one morning, making his way to Colorado before he was arrested again. He was a good-hearted man, but he struggled with addiction to heroin and really didn't know what to do with himself, in prison or out.

Campbell was being accompanied by Capt. Roger Seed, a prison official. Seed said that after the plane crashed, he jumped out of the rear exit, while Campbell stayed aboard, helping people out, calming them down, and reassuring them that they would be all right. Then Seed returned to the plane, and the two of them searched through the wreckage to see if they could find anyone else. But the danger of fire was looming, and the flight attendants had the two men leave the plane. So Captain Seed jumped out, followed by Kim Campbell.

But somehow the two men were separated as they escaped. Seed looked all over for Campbell, and Campbell looked all over for Seed. Campbell received some medical treatment for his back, and he even talked to one of the pilots. The pilot said he'd write a note about Campbell's rescue work and send it to the penitentiary—according to Campbell's mother, whom he called later that night. His mother hoped he would turn himself back in. But after the crash Campbell simply vanished.

For a doomed plane Flight 173 was lucky. The plane never did catch fire—the very cause of the crash, the lack of fuel, also allowed many to survive. There was some speculation that the pilot had deliberately run out its fuel to avoid a fiery crash. But the National Transportation Safety Board eventually found that Captain McBroom was simply so worried about the landing gear—which turned out to be fine—that he did not pay enough attention to the state of the fuel, and that his first officer and flight engineer failed to communicate their concerns about the fuel to the captain. Nevertheless, McBroom and his crew were able to maneuver the plane into a landing that saved as many lives as they could without killing anyone on the ground.

C H A P T E R 13

"THIS IS IT!"

The Eruption of Mount St. Helens

1980

Jim Scymanky was thinning Douglas fir trees just north of Mount St. Helens, near the north fork of the Toutle River. It was May 18, 1980, early in the morning, and he wanted to be 70 miles south, at home in Woodburn, Oregon. But instead he and the other three members of his crew—Jose Dias, Leonty Skorohodoff, and Evlanty Sharipoff, the foreman, all of whom lived in Woodburn—were up early, trying to finish their work. Together, they had been subcontracted to thin trees for Weyerhauser, the large timber company that owned some of the forest around Mount St. Helens. As Frank Parchman tells it in his book on the eruption of Mount St. Helens, *Echoes of Fury,* they had hoped to finish the day before, but there were a lot of trees to get through. Still, it was beautiful out in the woods—a perfect May morning, calm and cloudless, promising to be a warm and sunny day.

They were working in the shadow of the mountain. Like everyone else, of course, they had heard that the mountain could erupt at any time, but—also like many people—they didn't take the warnings that seriously. For one thing, they were miles outside the established "Red Zone," which was the official danger zone. And for another thing, in spite of the occasional steam venting, it just seemed improbable that something so large and so Pacific Northwest would blow up. Volcanoes erupted on Hawaii and other islands in the Pacific, or maybe Japan. Not here.

Mount St. Helens rises about 50 miles to the north of Portland, framing the visible landscape for the two million citizens of the greater Portland area. In 1980 its peak was perfectly symmetrical, a beloved destination for Oregonians, who worked and played there. It was renowned for its beauty—even William Clark, while traveling the Columbia River in 1805, commented in his journal that Mount St. Helens was "the most noble object in nature." The mountain had long been a favorite with recreators of every level, and it provided a livelihood for thousands, as well. All around the mountain were wild, lush forests and pristine lakes—especially Spirit Lake, the large lake just to the north of the peak. At Spirit Lake were camps and lodges, and all around the area were wonderful hiking trails that ran along cold mountain streams and up into the heights. It was an easy drive from Portland, and every weekend, dozens trekked up to the mountain for hiking, camping, and fishing.

Mount St. Helens is the youngest volcano in the Cascades, about 40,000 years old, and in 1980 its perfectly shaped peak was thought to be only about 2,500 years old, the result of dome-building activity after some great eruption in the past 3,000 years. Geologists knew it was an active volcano—that was evident from its native names alone: Lawelata (One from Whom Smoke Comes), Loo-wit (Keeper of the Fire), and Tah-one-lat-clah (Fire Mountain). And nineteenth-century witnesses describe the plumes of steam it sent into the air. But it had been silent for well over a century. On March 17, 1980, a small earthquake shook Mount St. Helens awake after this long slumber. One week later, the mountain spewed ash 2 miles into the air, the first major activity in more than a century. This minor eruption blew a hole in the top of the mountain, forming a crater 200 feet in diameter and 150 feet deep.

All throughout the spring, geologists, the news media, and curious citizens monitored the mountain as it steamed and shook. Government officials were worried enough that they evacuated homeowners in the vicinity and began to establish protected zones, setting up roadblocks to keep people from going beyond their borders. No one was quite sure what to expect. Geologists debated among themselves what it meant—would the mountain quiet down after these minor eruptions? Or would there be a major eruption that would send lava throughout the region? Based on the available science, there was good evidence for both scenarios. If there were an eruption, however, scientists guessed the mountain would spew ash or lava out of its center, giving people plenty of time to escape. So the Red Zone boundaries encircled the mountain itself, and not much beyond.

Like Scymanky and his co-workers, many Oregonians found it difficult to believe an eruption would actually take place at all. Weyerhauser employees were told it was perfectly safe outside the Red Zone, and people continued to work and play in the areas surrounding the mountain. Authorities set up roadblocks to keep tourists and campers a safe distance away, yet thousands of tourists flocked to the area, eager to see the mountain's continual explosions of steam. They drove right up to the roadblocks, joining a spontaneous fraternity of volcano watchers.

From March through May the mountain spewed ash and steam regularly, and earthquakes occurred with alarming frequency. Especially alarming was the unusual bulge forming on the north flank of the mountain. On May 10, more than twenty earthquakes were recorded on Mount St. Helens. But by May 15, the mountain seemed to have settled down, and the eruptions and earthquakes appeared to have stopped. Geologists who had gathered from all over the United States wondered whether they should go home. Tourists did go home—and those who had been forced out of their homes began to pressure government officials to let them go home too, or at least to retrieve some of their things. But even as the earthquakes calmed and the steam clouds waned, the north-flank bulge was growing ever larger, and at a steady and constant rate.

There's a photo of a bearded, bespectacled geologist, sitting in a camping chair, his long legs stretched out before him, resting on a log. He's wearing jeans and a green-and-blue rugby shirt. A green pickup and trailer are behind him and his notebook is in his lap. He is facing south. It's David Johnson, and he is grinning at the camera, and it's May 17, 1980, the afternoon before he's going to die.

David Johnson was one of the U.S. Geological Service volcanologists assigned to observe Mount St. Helens. He had had the overnight duty at the observation post 6 miles north of the mountain, substituting for his friend Don Swanson. The morning of May 18, he took his usual measurements. At 7 A.M., he radioed his most recent laser readings of the mountain to the Vancouver USGS station. The bulge was expanding at the same rate, and the gas emissions and temperature were in keeping with all the recent measurements.

At 8:32 on the morning of May 18, an earthquake measuring 5.1 on the Richter scale shuddered through Mount St. Helens. Witnesses report that the side of the mountain started to look fuzzy as ash began to spew out the top of the volcano. Then the bulge on the north flank simply melted away into one of the largest landslides ever known to occur. Mount St. Helens was erupting in a way no one had expected: a lateral blast out the north side of the mountain. David Johnson radioed his famous message: "Vancouver! Vancouver! This is it!" And then he fell silent.

According to Parchman, Jim Scymanky was busy with his trees. He was startled by Jose Dias, running toward him. Dias was yelling in Spanish: The volcano was exploding. Scymanky thought he was nuts—he hadn't heard anything like an explosion. He hadn't heard anything at all. But moments later, the four Oregon loggers did hear something: a great hiss that turned louder and louder as a cloud of gravel, rock, and ash roared over them. They had been caught in the lateral blast zone. Against all predictions, the mountain had not exploded up, but out, to the north.

The loggers turned to make a frantic escape. The trees they had cut blocked their route. Scymanky had only moved a few feet when he was knocked to the ground by some incredible force. Then the heat came. The men were buried in ash and suffered through a wave of heat that burned their bodies terribly. They choked on the hot, sticky ash. Volcanic ash is not like wood ash; rather, it is a very fine sand. This means it is extremely abrasive; it gets into everything and wants to stay there. If it gets into your lungs, it can scar them. Even worse, it can mix with your own mucus and turn into a kind of cement that chokes you to death.

Washington's greatest disaster, the eruption of Mount St. Helens, spewed a quarter inch of gritty ash over Portland, 50 miles south of the volcano.

USGS/CASCADES VOLCANO OBSERVATORY

Scymanky urged his friends to get to the stream that he had noticed earlier, about 25 yards from where they were. They crawled, in great pain, toward the water and immersed themselves for about half an hour. It was no longer the crystalline rivulet that he remembered—it was full of mud and ash. But at least it provided some relief from the fiery air.

The eruption obliterated everything in its direct blast zone, an area of about 8 miles in radius. The sheer force of the blast and its huge volume of debris killed or washed away everything in its path, leaving nothing but a moonscape of scree and ash. Beyond the direct blast zone lay an intermediate zone that extended nearly 20 miles. This zone was remarkable for and denoted by the giant trees that were mown down at the bottom of their trunks, miles and miles of them. The third zone was the seared zone; here, the gases from the blast didn't topple the trees, but it did singe them. The peak lost 1,300 feet to both the landslide and the explosive eruption. The landslide filled 24 square miles with debris. The lateral blast blew out 250 square miles of productive land. Spirit Lake had received so much debris from the landslide that it created a giant, 900-foot wave, spilling into its river systems and emptying the lake. Two hundred million cubic yards of ash, rock, mud, and debris were sent rushing into river channels. Mudflows poured down the sides of the mountain, wiping out everything in their path. The ash plume shot into the air for more than nine hours, bolstered by explosion after explosion from within the mountain. This cloud, composed of ash and steam, stretched 60,000 feet into the air, moving east at 60 miles per hour. Eventually, 540 million tons of ash blanketed an area covering more than 22,000 square miles.

Just after 8:30, people as far south as Newport, Oregon, and as far north as Vancouver, British Columbia, heard a powerful boom. "There goes Mount St. Helens," joked many, only finding out later, to their surprise, that they were right. They could hear the blast, but since they couldn't see anything, they assumed it was a sonic boom or some kind of explosion. Scymanky and the other people close to the volcano could see it but could not hear it. Near the mountain the blast was silent, but as the eruption sound waves radiated outward, they hit different temperatures, air currents, and land masses, and these collisions created the explosive sounds.

On this beautifully clear day in May, however, it was immediately evident from Portland what had happened: The top of the mountain was gone and a cloud of ash was pouring into the sky. All across the city plans for shopping, church, and sports events were abandoned, as Portlanders flocked to the places with the best views of Mount St. Helens. From Council Crest Park, the highest point in Portland, you could see the clouds of ash billowing eastward. The menacing plume of ash also created air turbulence—in essence it started its own weather system. It was possible to see lightning flashes against the black cloud.

The rest of Oregon took longer to sort out what had happened. If you could hear the blast from the Oregon coast, did that mean that the entire lower third of the state of Washington was obliterated? What about Portland? Was it the new Pompeii? Were streets flowing with lava? Many people were calling their loved ones in Portland, only to find out that, on a lazy Sunday morning, they were not yet even aware the mountain had erupted.

Up north, Scymanky, Dias, Skorohodoff, and Sharipoff knew they had to get off the mountain. All were severely burned. But they thought if they could get to their truck, then they'd be safe, so they left the stream and began walking toward where their truck was—or where it had been, anyway. The trees all around were seared black and ash was floating from the sky. They found the truck—it had been blown by the force of the blast into a ditch. At least they could get in it for shelter. Just as they reached the truck, a cloud of glowing, heated rock began to descend upon them. They couldn't open the back of the truck, so Scymanky yanked open the cab door and all four men painfully crowded their burned bodies into the cab, where they waited for the cloud to pass.

Scymanky was certain that this was the end for him. But after a while he got angry. He didn't want to die just sitting there in his truck. The latest ash cloud had passed—he wanted to get out of there. And so did the others. They made their way alongside the logging road, sticking close to the stream that the road followed, coughing and choking on ash, trying not to think about the intense pain they were suffering. Scymanky was worried that he and his friends were going into shock—they were all beginning to shiver as they walked. Scymanky was especially worried about Dias and Sharipoff, who were having a hard time staying with the other two and seemed to be delirious.

Eventually, they found their way was blocked by an enormous avalanche. On one side of the road was a cliff, and on the other a mountain rose straight up for a thousand feet. They were trapped. Sharipoff insisted on making his way back down the valley using another road they had seen. But Scymanky knew that would be death. The last place you want to be after a volcano erupts is in a river valley, vulnerable to heavy gasses and flooding. Scymanky could not stop his friend, though, and after yelling at him for a few minutes and trying to pull him back, he realized that he had to worry about saving himself. He walked back up toward the avalanche debris. There the remaining three drank from a spring that they had seen—it had clean water in it—and it was on higher ground. Maybe it would give them some chance of survival. Scymanky and Skorohodoff and Dias would drink from the spring, then would lie down in the warm ash to keep from shivering, and then get up and walk around when the pain from their burns was too much to bear.

They repeated this pattern for what seemed like hours. After some time Dias said he would go back to the avalanche and try to cross it. Scymanky tried to stop him, but Dias was determined, and Scymanky no longer had the strength to argue. So that left Scymanky and Skorohodoff. They lay there for a long time. Then they heard a new sound, even more terrifying: It was the hot mudflow roaring through the valley below them. They could see it—it was wide, as wide as several football fields, and it was consuming everything in its path, simply absorbing it. They watched it for a long time. It flowed past where they had seen Sharipoff, and they knew he was dead. They didn't know about Dias. They didn't know if the river of hot mud would rise high enough to consume them. They were becoming resigned to their own deaths.

Then Scymanky heard the helicopters. Maybe they were going to make it, after all.

The official death toll was fifty-seven, but it may have been higher. Not everyone registers with authorities, and the official Red Zone was well inside the area that was most affected by the blast. Most people died from breathing in the hot ash; others were instantly burned to death or buried in ash or mud.

Mount St. Helens continued to send steam and ash up into the sky for weeks and months after the first eruption. Its effects on Portland and Oregon were to come later—on June 12. That's when another eruption spewed the gritty ash over the metropolitan area. About a fourth of an inch spread throughout the Portland area, and south into nearby strawberry fields. Everything became coated in the stuff. People were told not to drive, since the ash can ruin engines, and many cars were simply abandoned at side of the road. There was a run on surgical masks and painter's face masks, and for the first time, Oregonians could feel and smell the effects of the eruption as well as see them. The strawberry crop—a major one in Oregon—was gone. Tourism and convention business was devastated, costing the economy tens of millions of dollars.

The costs to individual Oregonians was also high. Many of the fifty-seven official dead were from Oregon—families who had been camping or hiking, or people who had been working, like Sharipoff. Jim Scymanky did survive his injuries, but spent many years painfully recovering from them, suffering surgery after surgery. Skorodohoff was rescued, and Dias was also later found and rescued. But in spite of Scymanky's heroic efforts to save his friends, both died in the hospital after struggling for several months. Their burden of injuries was too great.

Like Scymanky, eventually the area around the mountain made something of a recovery, and the Mount St. Helens National Monument, with an impressive visitor center, nature recovery test sites, and other tourist attractions rose out of the ash. Thousands of tourists visit the mountain every year, impressed not only by the dramatic presentation of the events surrounding the eruption, but also by the miraculous recovery of the wildlife around it. If you go to Mount St. Helens today, you will reach a spot along Spirit Lake Memorial Highway that will take your breath away. After driving through lovely forests, suddenly the landscape changes. On the south side of the road lies a waste of gravel and ash. On the north side lie thousands and thousands of silver trees that appear to have been flattened in a nuclear holocaust. Indeed, the eruption of Mount St. Helens did have the force of several nuclear bombs. Yet continuing on, you will also reach a spot where wildlife has returned. Many of the large mammals were killed by the blast, but the things that they eat were not. Smaller animals burrowed. Plants eventually drifted back in. Today, the Mount St. Helens National Monument is a laboratory to study how the earth renews itself after catastrophe. If you travel to the end of the highway, you'll reach the Johnson Observatory—a masterpiece of story and science and a fitting tribute to the men and women who lost their lives in the disaster.

Mount St. Helens continued to have minor eruptions until 1984, when it fell silent. In January 1990 it sent a plume of steam into the air, but geologists didn't classify it as an eruption. They thought perhaps it was merely a snore, as the mountain settled back down to sleep. But on October 1, 2004, Mount St. Helens erupted again. Amazingly, after the eruption many Oregonians were drawn *toward* the mountain rather than away from it. One would have thought experience would be a better teacher, yet, as one witness remarked, "It may be dangerous, but the mountain is going to do what she is going to do, and you want to be a part of that." Across Portland we put down our work, standing at windows to watch. Schoolchildren wrote down their impressions and followed the television cameras that monitored the latest eruption.

Now, we Oregonians have gotten used to seeing Mount St. Helens with plumes of smoke and ash curling into the air, like a child's drawing of primitive islands with smoking volcanoes. She sends her signals regularly, warning us of the next eruption. The mountain is still thought of as a tourist attraction.

There are dangers we don't like to think about. Geologists have predicted that if an eruption and earthquake happened together, as they often do, Spirit Lake could entirely empty into the Toutle River. If that happened, the cities downriver would be wiped out. They also predict that this flooding would reach the Columbia River, and that the water and debris flow into the mighty Columbia could actually reverse the flow of the river. If that happened, they predict, the Portland area itself would flood. The loss of life would be tremendous. To forestall such a disaster, government engineers have strengthened the drainage tunnels around Spirit Lake. But a truly massive eruption would easily overwhelm existing engineering.

Mount St. Helens is now thought to be much more threatening than it was even ten years ago, at least in part because of its unpredictability. Will the mountain erupt again in such a devastating fashion? The answer is yes. The mystery is when.

CHAPTER 14

TRAGEDY ON MOUNT HOOD

The Oregon Episcopal School Climb

1986

On May 12, 1986, at 2 A.M., nineteen people set off from Timberline Lodge for a day climb of Mount Hood from the southern approach. It was a gray day on the mountain, but the climbers, who had been training for weeks to make this climb, were excited.

Most of them were high school sophomores and part of a project known as Basecamp, a wilderness education experience that was a major piece of the curriculum at Oregon Episcopal School. Oregon Episcopal School is a small private K–12 school, but it was internationally known for Basecamp. It was a very popular program—parents, students, and teachers loved it, for it was designed to teach leadership skills, responsibility, and preparedness, inarguably important things to know. Basecamp was required for graduation, and the Mount Hood climb was a key component. Students had to make the climb or perform forty hours of community service, and most chose the climb. They didn't have to make the summit, but they were required to endure the entire training course and go at least part way up with a fully loaded backpack. That year, the students included Erin O'Leary, Molly Schula, Erik Sandvik, Courtney Boatsman, Lorca Fitschen, Hilary Spray, Patrick McGinness, Tasha Amy, Brinton Clark, Richard Haeder, Susan McClave, and Giles Thompson.

They were led by forty-two-year-old Reverend Thomas Goman. Since 1977 he had directed the sophomore year of the Basecamp program. He was, by all accounts, a meticulous and expert climber, thoroughly dedicated to the safety of his students. He trained his students with hours of conditioning climbs. He taught them how to use ice axes, carabiners, ropes, harnesses. He taught them how to conserve body temperature and energy and the essential skills for wilderness survival. He made sure they had lots of socks—if their boots went on easily at home, they weren't wearing enough of them. Three pairs were required, along with plenty of layers of clothing, extra food, and spare pairs of gloves. Goman would not let students board the bus unless all of their equipment was inspected.

They needed to be well trained because Mount Hood can be treacherous—subject to sudden storms, whiteouts, and avalanches; prone to hidden crevasses and dangerous precipices. It is not for the foolhardy or the unprepared. But it is well traveled and thus a good climb for the novice. Goman himself had made the climb numerous times, most recently a couple of weeks earlier, to check out the route and make sure he had backup plans in case the weather turned. Late spring is a popular time to climb Mount Hood—the bad winter weather has passed, avalanche season is over, but there's still enough ice to keep boulders in place so they don't come crashing down on you.

Many climbers have been lost on the slopes of Mount Hood.
PHOTO COURTESY PORTLAND DEVELOPMENT COMMISSION

Like most parties, the Oregon Episcopal School climbers started out in the wee hours of the morning. An early departure allows groups to be at the summit at sunrise, so that they can return before the snow warms and melts a little, loosening rocks that could fall on them. They had their equipment. They had a snow shovel. They even had a pair of skis, carried by their assistant guide, Ralph Summers. They were well clad, in long underwear, heavy pants, sweaters, parkas, and thick boots—as well as all those socks.

The morning began fair enough, and for much of it the climbing was good. Still, several students turned back. Hilary

Spray and her mother had returned—Hilary had become ill, perhaps from altitude sickness. After a while Courtney Boatsman noticed that her friend Lorca Fitschen was crying, doubled over with pain from an old injury that the climb was exacerbating. Courtney herself was achy—her own back already was sore from throwing the javelin at track-and-field practice. So she was not entirely unhappy when Tom Goman asked if she could shepherd Lorca back down the mountain.

When they reached Timberline Lodge, Courtney and Lorca watched their friends and teachers as they continued up the mountain. Then, when the group was almost at the summit, clouds rolled in and the two girls couldn't see them any more.

Meanwhile, Summers and Goman halted the group at the climbers' way station, Silcox Hut, to figure out what to do about Marion Horwell. She was the dean of the upper-grade students, and while an excellent sport, she was not an experienced climber, and she was having some trouble breathing. Mount Hood doesn't require extra oxygen to climb it, but it can be difficult if one is not used to carrying a lot of weight at that altitude. Goman decided to press on—they weren't that far from the summit, and they should at least make an attempt.

But beginning at 4 P.M., the weather suddenly turned bad—very bad. At first it was just cold, wet, and windy. The climbers struggled on for about an hour, but by then one student, Patrick McGinnis, was beginning to show signs of hypothermia. They had reached the Hogback, a ridge about 1,000 feet below the summit. Summers and Goman conferred again. They decided that conditions were getting dangerous and that the group should turn back.

That's when the blizzard hit. Howling winds of 30 to 50 knots blew around them. Patrick had begun to shudder from hypothermia, and the party had to stop to warm him. They wrapped him in a sleeping bag, and someone even got inside with him and that got him to stop shaking. But he could still not walk on his own.

At the 8,000-foot level, Summers realized they were off course and stopped the group. In reality they were near White River Canyon, and if they had just pressed on a little farther, they could have made it back to camp. But they couldn't tell where they were because of the whiteout conditions. Student Molly Schula remembered, "There was no distinction between the sky and snow."

Faced with the danger before them, Summers and Goman decided to dig a snow cave—a decision that later proved controversial. But they had a kid with hypothermia who couldn't walk, and if they continued their descent without being able to see, they could get so far off course that they would be in danger of falling over a precipice or into a crevasse. So those who were capable got down to work. They had only one snow shovel, and they had to dig a lot of the cave by hand. Most of the kids were suffering, and they sat trying to warm themselves under a tarp. When the cave was complete, they put their backpacks under the tarp and crawled in.

The snow shovel blew away.

The door to the snow cave was fit with a yellow tarpaulin. Inside, Brinton Clark was afraid. The cave was small—really—it was big enough to hold two people, and there were thirteen of them inside. And it wasn't that warm. During the long night that followed, the climbers tried to keep up their spirits and talk each other through the ordeal. But there was also a lot of crying. The snow cave was claustrophobic. The students and their teachers and guide were packed in tightly, and sometimes people panicked and tried to leave the cave. Panicked or not, Ralph Summers said that they had to leave every once in awhile to get fresh air. But the entrance was buried by shifting snow, so whenever climbers went out, they had to clear thick snow from the entrance to the cave. A couple of times, students left to retrieve their backpacks, which contained supplies that could keep them all warmer. But the cold was so disorienting that they forgot why they had left the cave.

By the next morning, Ralph Summers knew that things were bad. He crawled out of the small cave entrance into the raging blizzard. He made his way to the tarp, thinking of his skis. He obviously couldn't ski anywhere in them, but he could use them to mark the entrance to the snow cave in case anyone was searching for them. But the tarp was buried under the snow, and he could feel the cold, blowing wind draining his strength as he struggled to uncover the skis. Summers returned to the cave and told Goman he was going for help.

The mood in the cave was dire, and the climbers were losing hope. They were cold and wet. But they were still healthy. Summers asked Giles Thompson to go with him, but Giles wouldn't leave. Instead, Molly Schula volunteered. She was strong, and Summers knew she could do it. She told her teacher, Father Tom, that she was leaving. He said, listlessly, "Molly, good-bye." After they left, Brinton said, the entrance to the cave gradually filled with snow. As it got smaller, all the people in the snow cave knew they were going to die.

Ralph and Molly struggled through the canyon in heavy snow. Amazingly, they found the snow shovel a little bit below the cave. But they decided it would be too risky to climb back up and return it—it would drain them of strength and take too much time. So they kept on, fighting blizzard winds so strong they blew the two to the ground, across White River Canyon. They had a compass, yet they still lost their way now and then. But then all at once, they found themselves in the Meadows Ski Area, under the chairlift.

Molly said, "Oh, God, we're saved."

Summers shook his head. "No, Molly. We have to wait until everyone is with us to celebrate."

Ralph Summers was an experienced climber and teacher. He was thirty years old and a guide from the Pacific Crest Outward Bound School. While his role was not to lead this hike—and so he deferred to Goman—he felt entirely responsible for every one of the kids in the cave. He threw himself into the rescue effort that had started Monday. On Tuesday, May 13, with the arrival of Schula and Summers, the search picked up tremendously. For most of Tuesday, rescuers used snowcats and helicopters to search the mountain, making pass after pass over the area where the climbers were thought to be. Other teams were using dogs and metal detectors. All efforts were halted when another storm blew in, with 60-mile-per-hour winds and a windchill of fifty below zero.

Early Wednesday morning, rescue efforts began again. And at 6 A.M. a helicopter crew from the Air Force Reserve found three of the students: Erin, Alison, and Erik. They had left the cave in the night, apparently to seek help. Sgt. Richard Harder found two of them at about 7,700 feet, spying them from the air, and then ground crews found the third student about 500 yards away, at 8,200 feet. They were airlifted out immediately while paramedics, and later, hospital crews, attempted to revive them. These efforts were halted on the girls on Wednesday afternoon. Erik died at 5:30 that evening.

Back at the mountain more than one hundred searchers were combing the hillsides, knowing that time was rapidly running out. The rescue team worked late into the evening, but then more bad weather rushed in and arrested their search.

On Thursday the helicopter sweeps continued, as did the ground searches. Summers was frustrated. He was with a group at the 8,300-foot level on the south side of the mountain, near White River Canyon. Still, nothing looked familiar—the storm had changed the look of the terrain. Toward the evening, the group of twenty-three searchers was called back in. They were planning to stop at 5 P.M.; clouds were starting to roll in yet again. They decided to make one last pass, when they noticed something. It was the yellow tarpaulin.

They heard a faint voice. The rescue crews began digging frantically. Meanwhile, the triage nurses and paramedics arrived on scene and were ready the moment the rescue crew broke through the snow cave.

Two climbers were on top of the pile of bodies in the snow cave: Brinton and Giles. They were too cold to talk, but they were alive and conscious.

People with hypothermia are at great risk of injury, so the rescue team had to work slowly and gently. The helicopters were brought in, and they flew all eight survivors to Portland hospitals. Susan McCleve's body temperature was thirty-nine degrees; she died before she reached the hospital. Patrick McGinness's temperature was fifty-four degrees, and he died later that evening. Marion Horwell also died that evening, as did Tasha Amy, Richard Haeder—and Tom Goman. But Brinton Clark and Giles Thomson survived.

Afterward, everyone wanted to know what went wrong. Oregon Episcopal School, which had suffered terrible human losses—nine students, two faculty members, as well as its beloved Basecamp program—had also lost a half-million dollar lawsuit over the disaster. It appointed a commission of national climbing experts to study what happened. It all came down to timing, equipment, and leadership. Sticking to a schedule is a virtue in the classroom, but perhaps not so much on wilderness adventures. Having to stick to the schedule meant that the climbers were reluctant to change their plans no matter what the forecast. Likewise, they found that students really didn't have enough things to keep them warm and carried no altimeter or topographical map. Leadership was also a problem. While Summers was thoroughly exonerated in court and by the students, he deferred to Goman's leadership even when some students wanted to go back—and he knew they were right. Still, Goman himself was an expert climber and a figure of authority, so it's not surprising that Ralph Summers deferred to his judgment.

The snow cave was also criticized as being poorly designed and as an option to which they resorted too soon. But again, snow caves have been known to save lives. In 1975 a snow cave saved the lives of three Portland teenagers. They had left for a climb of the summit on Mount Hood on New Year's Eve. Matt Meacham, Randy Knapp, and Gary Schneider took three days to reach the summit, and then on their descent, they got lost and fell into a crevasse. In the meantime terrible weather descended upon them. They built a snow cave and survived on pudding and pancake mix and Bible reading for two weeks, until the raging blizzard stopped and they could walk out. They had to dig themselves out from under 40 feet of snow, but they were not otherwise harmed.

Only one other glaciated peak—Japan's Mount Fuji—is thought to be climbed more often than Mount Hood, and 10,000 people make the Mount Hood climb each year. Sometimes climbers cause their own traffic jams at the summit. But this popularity belies the danger. Mount Hood was the site of the first recorded death, in 1896, in modern climbing, and since then scores of people have lost their lives on the mountain.

C H A P T E R 1 5

BURNING FIELDS

Chain-Reaction Car Accident

1988

This is the story of a terrible chain-reaction car accident in 1988, the kind that is common in the West. Oregon is subject to periodic dust storms, and in 1999 blowing dust blinded drivers along Interstate 84 near Pendleton, causing a fiery crash that killed eight. The cloud was caused by a freak windstorm brought on by low pressure that took up the dust left by a farmer plowing his fields. One trucker saw the cloud, turned around, and started back down the road to warn oncoming traffic. The other drivers just thought his waves were friendly; they waved back and kept straight on into the deadly cloud.

Fifty cars and trucks were involved in that accident. The dust had been blowing, but the visibility, while poor, seemed not to deter the speed of the drivers. When everything went black, cars and trucks in the eastbound lane plowed into one another. It was so dark drivers stopping to help could not even see the car fires burning. They could only feel them.

Nobody really blamed anyone for the dust storm—they are known to happen from time to time in the area. In fact, in 1931 a dust storm frothed up in eastern Oregon eventually made it all the way across the Cascades and out to the Pacific. It looked as though a volcano had erupted. Observers at the time estimated the amount of dust in the air would fill thirty-three boxcars. So, while deadly and unwelcome, dust storms are accepted with a certain amount of fatalism. They just happen.

But on August 3, 1988, things were different. This accident occurred just south of Albany, on Interstate 5, on a stretch of freeway that is perpetually under construction. The freeway there spans four lanes, two in each direction, and it cuts through the fertile farmland of the southern Willamette Valley; farms have been there for generations. It was and is a congested strip of freeway, filled with people in a hurry to travel to and from the cities along the Willamette River—Eugene, Albany, Corvallis, Salem, Portland—on various kinds of urgent business.

The Willamette Valley has been prime grassland for thousands of years. Before it was farmed by pioneer settlers, native tribes had been good stewards of the grassland, letting it burn or even burning it deliberately to ensure good grazing for the game that kept them alive through the winter (as well as a way to flush out the game in the autumn). Indeed, field burning is one of the most long-standing agricultural practices known to human beings, and it is still used worldwide. In the 1930s, Willamette Valley farmers discovered that grass for lawns grew beautifully in the damp climate, and after World War II, the grass-seed farming business really took off, as the post-Depression, postwar boom for houses also meant a great demand for lawns. Americans have a passion for wide, green lawns, and today two-thirds of the world's grass seed is grown in this valley. Then, in the 1940s, agronomists at Oregon State University suggested that the grass-seed farmers revive the ancient practice of burning their fields. Sure, it was messy and irritating, but nothing was as effective for getting rid of weeds and disease, as well as for enriching the soil. It was carefully controlled, with permits granted on the basis of many things, including prevailing winds.

But fire cannot always be controlled and winds are not always predictable. On August 3, 1988, seven people died in a hideous accident when smoke from a farmer's field drifted across the freeway.

Farmer Paul Stutzman of Albany, who owned the field, was burning eighty-two acres of grass that day. He was authorized to burn the field starting at 3 P.M. The field for which Stutzman actually received the permit did not lie next to the freeway. The sequence of events is not entirely clear, but it is surmised that as Stutzman was working his field, embers from the controlled burn blew into the next field over. The winds were not supposed to be strong that day, but when it comes to Oregon weather, anything can happen. And even the slightest breeze or dust devil could send sparks flying.

The fire in the nearby field was soon out of control, generating thick black clouds of smoke. These clouds drifted over the freeway. And before anyone could do anything, at 4 P.M. twenty-one cars and trucks had piled on top of one another in a shocking crash that would sear the imagination of Oregonians for a long time.

Events happened so quickly that it was hard to know exactly what happened. Truck driver Kevin Sterba was driving a wood-chip truck—slowly, with the lights turned on, since smoke was limiting what he could see. Suddenly, he said, there was a big black cloud of smoke that was absolutely blinding. A dairy truck driver said he could see for about 100 yards; then all at once, he was engulfed by darkness. Somehow, he was able to drive between the chip truck and another car. Then he climbed out of his truck and into an inferno. Trucks were on fire. Cars were on fire. People were crawling through the grass on the side of the freeway and running from the flames. Then, said another survivor, there was nothing but "glass busting, metal crushing, and screaming."

The accident closed the freeway for nearly 8 miles. The survivors of the accident and the people who stopped to help them said it looked like a war zone: Everywhere was black smoke, burnt grass. Trucks were blown out and charred, as if they had been in a bombed-out area. Cars were so twisted from the fire that it was difficult to distinguish one from another. Ten cars and trucks caught fire and thirty-seven people were injured.

Nearby, in Albany, people were starting to realize what had happened. Dale Cronin, a factory manager near the scene of the accident, told his employees to bring first-aid kits, food, water. On site the Oregon State Patrol, paramedics, fire trucks, and ambulances clogged the road.

Paula George was driving north with her six children, ages one to ten, when she encountered the cloud of smoke. She wasn't sure what it was—it seemed to be fog, so she slowed down and turned on her lights. But suddenly, it was impossible to see anything. She stopped altogether. She turned toward the backseat to check on the children, make a joke, and calm them down. Just as suddenly, the van was hit from behind. Then it was hit again . . . and again, over and over as the cars piled up behind her.

The van was on fire. The four oldest children got out without any trouble, but the two little ones were in grave danger. She struggled to get her baby, Jaclyn, age one and a half, out of the car seat. Finally, she just gave up, unbuckled the car seat, and threw it, with Jaclyn still buckled in, out of the van. But the baby landed too close to the van for her to be safe—she was in reach of the flames that had just started to shoot up. So Paula climbed out of the van, leaving two-year-old Johnny buckled in his car seat, and grabbed the baby off the ground. She jumped through the fire with Jaclyn and ran away from the van, where a man saw her and took the baby from her to bring her to a safe place.

Paula looked at the van, with Johnny still inside. A wall of fire surrounded the vehicle, and of course she was afraid. But she moved quickly toward him. Right behind her was her oldest son Paul, age ten. He was worried about his mom and brother; he could see they needed help. They got Johnny out of his car seat and plunged back through the flames to safety. Finally, Paula looked at Johnny and realized with horror that his face had been terribly burned. The skin was coming off it in places. And Paul had burned his legs and feet. But they were safe, and they were going to make it.

Seven people didn't make it. One boy, an eight-year-old named Travis Trujillo, was thrown from his family's pickup truck. The victims also included an entire family—the daughter of writer William Wharton, Kathleen; her husband, William Rodewald; and their daughters Dayiel, age two, and Mia, eight months. The family was burned to death in their van, their bodies charred beyond recognition. They were traveling from their home in rural Oregon to a wedding in Portland.

Wharton and his wife flew out to Oregon after the accident. They tried to find out what had befallen their beautiful daughter and her wonderful family. He even photographed their burned bodies, hoping to find some answers or receive some kind of closure. But such an event is never really over. Wharton was indignant that a farmer would use a "barbaric" technique such as field burning, and he spent many years trying to have the practice banned.

Many Willamette Valley residents agreed, having had to tolerate summer days filled with black smoke visible for 50 miles in every direction, the acrid smell of burning grass, and flames that were sometimes 500 feet in the air. Many felt it had just been a matter of time before something like this happened. Traffic was forever getting heavier on the freeway, people driving faster all the time, and they were not going to change their driving habits to suit the grass-seed farmers.

But banning field burning outright was not going sit well with farmers who relied on the practice to sanitize their fields—and who are a substantial economic engine for Oregon. The Oregon legislature, trying to make everyone happy, did not ban the practice, but they did set ever more stringent limits on open field burning, so that only about 10 percent of total acres can be burned in any year. Farmers were forced to rethink their practices. They voluntarily reduced the amount of burning by 80 percent. They found that some varieties of grass did not need burning and were fine without it. And they discovered that there was an international market for the baled straw from the leftover grass-seed harvest.

Still, summer days in the Willamette can still be blanketed by clouds of thick smoke. Its hideous acrid smell should remind us of the cost of our wide green lawns.

CHAPTER 16

A WET AND WILD WINTER

Raging Waters

1995–1996

The story of the 1996 floods begins in November 1995, after Thanksgiving. On the 28th, western Oregon was inundated by a fierce rainstorm that filled rivers throughout the area. The Clackamas River flooded. The ZigZag River flooded. The Wilson River near Tillamook flooded, and the city was cut off when two mudslides closed the road. People said that the only time the rivers were higher was back during the Christmas Day flood of 1964.

On December 9, a severe ice storm shut down western Oregon. Trees fell onto houses. Travelers were stranded on Interstate 84. Cars went off the road everywhere. Schools were closed, and so were many businesses—though not all of them. One woman called her boss and said, "I'm afraid I can't get in." Her boss said, "Don't be afraid. Just get in."

On December 12, a small hurricane blew through western Oregon, causing millions of dollars in damage. Trees that easily withstood the Columbus Day Storm now sank to the ground. Roofs flew off buildings all over the state in the 74-mile-per-hour winds. The gusts of 90 miles per hour ruined a few more trees and houses and helped sink boats moored along the Columbia River.

On January 18, and then again on January 27, came the snows—which in western Oregon means everything grinds to a halt. In the eastern part of the state, Oregonians deal with snow with equanimity, but west of the Cascades, snowstorms send local news anchors into a frenzy of live reports and dramatic coverage of cars abandoned at the sides of the roads and children sledding down hillsides.

The snow also fell in the Cascades, which was good. Oregon relies on the snowpack to provide water during dry summers, and by January 1996, the snowpack was much lower than average, by about 29 percent, and the climatologists were beginning to worry about drought. But so much snow fell in the last half of January that the snowpack surpassed the norm—by 12 percent.

On February 2, the jet stream moved south, bringing with it ice-cold air from northern Canada. The rivers had ice in them for the first time in decades. In eastern Oregon temperatures plunged below zero. In western Oregon the windchill was minus twenty degrees. And it had begun to rain—rain that froze as it reached the cold, snowy ground, coating everything in thick sheets of ice. Daily life ground to a halt.

On February 5, it began to thaw and local rivers were noticeably higher.

On February 6, the rains came—and knowing what happens when warm winds from the Pacific blow through after a big ice storm, people started filling the sandbags.

In Oregon we have two major kinds of flooding: rural and urban. Rural flooding happens when lots of rain and snowmelt inundate streams and rivers, causing them to spill over their banks. This is a natural process, and while inconvenient—and even occasionally deadly—this kind of flooding is a reason that the Willamette Valley is so fertile, for it deposits soil and minerals onto the valley floor. But urban flooding is like rural flooding on steroids. Parking lots, streets, and driveways mean that the water has nowhere to go.

The rainstorm of February 6 came north from the Equator, bringing a great deal of rain—record amounts of rain, in fact. And this storm lasted longer than usual, for several days. On the Oregon coast Newport was inundated with nearly 8 inches of rain in three days, while 23 inches fell on Laurel Mountain. In Eugene more than 5 inches of rain fell in one day.

But the amount of rainfall was only half the problem. The other half was that it was warm. It was warm like a June night. It never got below fifty degrees. With great suddenness the mountain freezing levels were at 8,000 feet instead of 3,000. The roads across the mountain passes were slick under warm spring rains, arriving months early. Snow began to melt.

The water had to go somewhere, and by February 6, streams across the mountain ranges of Oregon had reached flood level. The McKenzie River, which flows out of the Cascades west toward Eugene, had five times as much water flowing through its dams on the 6th than it did on the 5th. As small streams and large filled with rain and melting snow, they spilled over their banks and began washing down the hillsides and onto the valley floor.

At first local authorities said that the Willamette and Columbia Rivers probably wouldn't flood—that the local streams and smaller tributary rivers likely would, but that the large rivers could absorb the extra volume. But as the rains kept falling, they got out their one-hundred-year flood chronologies and noticed that floods happen rather more often here: 1861, 1894, 1923, 1948, 1964. All along beautiful Oregon rivers—the McKenzie, the Sandy, the Mollala, the Clackamas, the Tualatin, the ZigZag—people watched as the waters rose with great rapidity to levels even greater than in 1964. One elderly woman along the Tualatin River in Washington County, west of Portland, remarked, "I don't think it will flood. It never did before, but if it does, well—that's what's going to happen."

By February 7, it had happened.

Driving from Portland to Eugene along Interstate 5 was like driving over a 106-mile-long bridge spanning a glassy pond. By the next day, Oregon was in danger. Along the Santiam River, east of Salem, sheriffs took inflatable boats around to evacuate 3,000 stranded residents. In Oregon's capital, Salem, Mill Creek ran over the tops of its bridges. In Scio livestock was endangered. Horses were trapped on one farm, injuring themselves in a desperate attempt to escape rising waters. They were attempting to kick down fences. The horses were rescued and taken to nearby farms. But not everyone was as lucky. An eight-year-old girl from Scio, Amber Bargfreele, was drowned when she went out to get the mail, swept away into a flooded culvert.

As was the case in the 1964 flood, Mount Hood communities suffered greatly. Thirty-five people and two dogs along the Columbia River Gorge, west of Cascade Locks, were rescued by the National Guard. They were trapped by two severe mudslides along I–84 that buried two cars. The residents watched as the hillsides moved before their eyes. Along the Sandy River, Don Boswell saw Harold Jenk, a seventy-year-old man, and his wife Jackie standing on the roof of their house—which had been swept into the river. Harold was rescued, but Jackie was lost to the roiling waters.

In Portland the Willamette was at 21 feet, while the flood stage is set at 18 feet. Weather authorities predicted the river would go higher—maybe as high as 28 feet, which would put it over the top of the seawall that lines the river through downtown Portland, thus jeopardizing thousands of businesses and homes. Mayor Vera Katz ordered the sandbagging to start; city workers ordered the sand and plywood.

By February 8, the Willamette was at 24 feet in downtown Portland. Hundreds of volunteers arrived to help save the downtown area. It was a moving display of community spirit. People just showed up, and from all over the Northwest. One man hitchhiked all the way from Idaho. He felt he couldn't stand by and do nothing. A woman from Seattle, Linda Swearingen, was simply stuck in town due to road closings; she thought *what the heck?* and stayed to work alongside everyone else. Another man, Jim Reynolds, sandbagged every day. At eighty-three he had had both knees replaced, and he was working out a mighty grief—his wife had died in a terrible car accident the previous December. Working alongside the hundreds of volunteers seemed to ease the pain a little.

After two days of sandbagging and carpentry, Portland had extended its seawall by several feet, using 2 miles of plywood and 45,000 bags of sand. The peak of the flood occurred on February 9 and 10.

But while downtown was safe, the rest of the city was contending with moving, rumbling earth. Skyline Boulevard, a drive that winds its way along the top of the hills through the most expensive real estate in the city, lost a 70-foot stretch of road. It simply collapsed, taking two cars along with it and creating a pit that was 50 feet deep. The drivers were unhurt, thanks to one brave firefighter, Dan Bremer. Here was a man who rescued people from burning buildings and other dire situations. But to save the two drivers, he had to rappel down the writhing hillside and was nearly buried himself. He told the *Oregonian* that he now had "a new definition of fear."

As always, the worst losses occurred along the Oregon coast, especially the low-lying pasturelands near Tillamook. Record rainfall had hit the coast range above Tillamook, and now the water was pouring down the mountain creeks and rivers. The dairy farms of Tillamook are responsible for some of the nation's finest cheese, ice cream, and yogurt, but the same qualities that make it excellent grazing for cows make it vulnerable to flooding. Five rivers flow into Tillamook Bay, as do four large streams. The lush pasturelands were transformed into soggy sponges and then buried under several feet of mud. Farmers tried to move their cattle to higher ground, but many drowned, and the cries of the desperate animals were sickening to hear.

During the flood Tillamook was completely cut off from the world. The major highway, U.S. Highway 101, was blocked by water and landslides, as was the major road leading to the interior of the state, Oregon 6, which follows the normally peaceable Wilson River. Dozens of motorists were caught off guard; their cars began filling with water, and they had to escape out windows. Hundreds of residents were stranded—unless they fled while they still could—by the 6 feet of water that covered US 101.

Flooding is not novel for Tillamook, but it was more rapid here, and the water was higher than in other parts of the state. The Wilson River was at its highest recorded level ever, at 18.5 feet. The damage to Tillamook County eventually reached $53 million in losses that were not covered by insurance. Seven hundred dairy cows drowned. Dozens of houses and businesses were obliterated by the water.

People in Tillamook County are not rich, but they know how to work hard. After the flood citizens and county officials met with state and federal planners to figure out how to rebuild more safely. They knew that the floods would come again. Together, they elevated more than fifty houses and fourteen businesses. They built five cow pads, which could be used as shelters for cows that might be stranded by future floods. Three and a half years later, their plans were tested: It rained more than 9 inches on Thanksgiving Day, severely flooding the area. But this time, no cows were lost. And none of the elevated houses were flooded.

In some ways all flood stories are similar: too much of a good thing. The element we rely on to give us life betrays us, destroying home and livelihood. If we're lucky, we'll live through them. If we're even luckier, like the residents of Tillamook, a flood will give us an opportunity for renewal.

CHAPTER 17

COOS BAY CATASTROPHE

The Wreck of the *New Carissa*

1999

West of Astoria, in the sands of Clatsop Beach, lies the rusting skeleton of the *Peter Iredale,* a ship that ran aground in 1906, caught by an October squall. No one was injured, but all attempts at salvaging the ship were fruitless, and it was abandoned to the elements—and to the tourists. For a century the wreck has been visited and photographed, since it is an easy walk at low tide. Farther south another such memorial can be found in Boiler Bay. The boiler in question belonged to the *J Marhoffer,* which caught fire and foundered among the rocks 14 miles north of Yaquina Bay in 1910. The boiler of the ship broke free and stayed in the bay for years and years, popping in and out of the breakers, taunting all who tried to remove it.

The latest example of such marine stubbornness is the *New Carissa,* a 639-foot freighter that was registered to a Panamanian shipping company. In 1999, on the evening of February 3, the *New Carissa* was approaching Coos Bay, empty and waiting to receive its cargo. It had been sent from Japan to fetch 37,000 tons of wood chips.

The wreck of the New Carissa *in the shallow waters north of Coos Bay Harbor was an environmental disaster.* COURTESY UNITED STATES COAST GUARD

But before it could actually enter the Coos Bay Harbor, it was caught up in a severe squall. The high winds and 26-foot swells meant that it was not safe for the pilot assigned to the ship to guide the *New Carissa* into port. It would have to wait until the next day. The ship turned away from the bay. Its crew opened the empty holds and anchored a mile and a half off shore. But in the thick of the storm, the ship's anchors were dragged across the ocean floor and the ship began to drift. Early in the morning, before sunrise, the *New Carissa* ran aground about 150 yards off a remote, sandy beach, 3 miles north of Coos Bay.

By 9 A.M. the next day, the Coast Guard station in North Bend, just to the south of the grounded ship, was alerted. They got right to work: When a ship that large is grounded, it likely has a lot of oil in it that might pose a danger to shore. The Coast Guard contacted various agencies and assembled a team, called the Unified Command team, which brought together the major government agencies and private companies that would be involved in the rescue and refloating of the *New Carissa*.

The first goal of the Unified Command was to make sure the crew was safe; the second was to refloat the ship; and the third, keep any oil from leaking. Achieving this first goal was difficult. The surf was heavy and dangerous and the winds were high. It took some heroic action for the rescue team to board the ship, but they managed to save all the crew.

The Unified Command then brought in a team by helicopter to assess the possibilities for refloating the ship. Refloating seemed achievable, but there were problems. One problem was that there were no salvage vessels in the area that were capable of pulling this giant ship off the sand. The closest was in Astoria, 170 miles away. The crew of the salvage vessel was contacted, and they made plans to head immediately for Coos Bay. But by then the winter storm that had grounded the *New Carissa* had also engulfed Astoria, so it took this ship—the *Salvage Chief*—two extra days to get to Coos Bay. Then, due to the delay of the *Salvage Chief*, the *New Carissa* had drifted 600 feet closer to shore—beyond the reach of the *Salvage Chief* when it finally arrived on February 9.

The Unified Command team had to reprioritize its goals. Now the primary goals were to ensure the safety of the salvage crew and the local community, to minimize the environmental damage—which had the potential to be severe—and finally, to salvage the *New Carissa*.

That brings us to the heart of the second problem: The *New Carissa* had 400,000 gallons of viscous oil in its fuel tanks, and the longer the ship was grounded, the greater the chance that this oil would leak. It ran aground near the South Slough National Estuarine Reserve, a wildlife reserve within Coos Bay. This is protected habitat for many marine species. It includes space for migratory shorebirds, seabirds, and marine mammals, and it contains within it extensive tidal flats, teeming with life.

By February 9, the *New Carissa* had suffered through five days of pounding by the surf and it was beginning to show. The ship had started to leak, and small tarballs of escaped oil began to appear on the ocean and drift toward shore. This triggered an intensive response to the spill, and volunteers from across Oregon came to help clean the beach and the birds.

Another severe storm was predicted for the next day, February 10. Unified Command faced a dilemma. If they tried to pull the ship off the sand right away, it would probably breach the hull and spill the remaining fuel—more than 300,000 gallons. If they waited for the storm, the outcome was wholly unpredictable, but most likely devastating to the coastline.

The ship had already been declared a total loss. So they decided to burn the *New Carissa* to get rid of the remaining fuel. The environmental groups in charge of the beach cleanup were unhappy, but they agreed that if nothing was done, there was sure to be a mighty spill. They had already lost several thousand shorebirds. Still, it was a risky and controversial decision. By way of defending it, the authors of a federal report on the disaster quote Theodore Roosevelt: "In any moment of decision, the best thing you can do is the right thing, the next best thing is the wrong thing, and the worst thing is nothing."

At least they didn't do that.

Burning a ship at sea, on purpose, especially in high surf, is not an easy thing to do. There had never before been an attempt to perform a controlled burn such as this one in the contiguous forty-eight states. The first attempt failed, but the next day, on February 11, an expert navy team placed 400 pounds of explosives onboard. The explosives, along with a "locally brewed" mixture of napalm and other things, successfully ignited the fire. Sticky clouds of black smoke filled the air, prompting spectators statewide to wonder whether the fire was such a good idea, but the fire managed to burn off approximately half of the ship's fuel.

Things looked twice as good for the local wildlife, but how were they going to get rid of the other half of the fuel? Complicating things even more, the burned ship had now broken in half, split between the bow and the stern. And the two halves of the ship were drifting apart in the strong current, releasing oil.

Most of the oil was in the bow half. The Unified Command team decided to send the bow section 248 miles offshore with a special, extra-long towline that had to be flown in from Holland. Out that far, they could sink the bow. There the water was very deep and cold, and the oil would likely be trapped there forever, congealed in the bow. But in the meantime the goal was to get as much oil off that ship as possible—difficult to do, given the consistency of the oil. It was decided that, because of the urgency of the situation, it would be best to pump it off and store it in onshore containers. The salvage crew worked through heavy seas to pump 110,000 gallons off the ship. But when they examined this fuel, it turned out to be mostly seawater.

Nevertheless, the towing procedures went ahead as planned. On February 23, a helicopter tried to hook the special towline from the tugboat *Sea Victory* to the orphaned bow of the *New Carissa*. This frustrating experience was repeated over the next three days, thwarted by the wind and seas. By February 26, the crew got a break in the weather and the tides and managed to inch the bow off the sand and into the sea—a process that took another three days. On March 1, the bow was finally freed and began its journey to its watery grave. Joining in this procession was the *Oregon Responder,* an oil-skimmer, to ensure that any leaking oil would be safely contained.

The bow of the *New Carissa* apparently had a different idea about her fate, however. Yet another winter storm blew in on March 2, this one a hurricane registering 90-mile-per-hour winds, accompanied by seas that were 30 feet high. The *Oregon Responder* had to turn back. Then the *New Carissa* broke free of her towline, 50 miles out to sea, and once again drifted toward shore. It ended up this time to the north of Coos Bay, at Waldport.

No one could believe it. Once again, beach cleanup crews were alerted. Waldport's marine life, if anything, was more sensitive than that at Coos Bay. It is the home of three endangered bird species—the marbled murrelet, the peregrine falcon, and the bald eagle. In addition, the value of the commercial oyster farms and other fishing in the area, all of which require oil-free water, ran into the millions of dollars. Oregonians held their breath wondering if the bow of the *New Carissa* would keep her cargo to herself.

Finally, after several more winter storms, on March 8, the *Sea Victory* was able to pull the *New Carissa* safely off the beach at Waldport and out to sea. This time she stayed attached for the entire 280 miles. On March 11, the Coast Guard and the navy placed 380 pounds of plastic explosives in the bow of the *New Carissa*. Even that didn't sink the ship's carcass. Finally, the navy shot an MK-48 torpedo at the ship. It was a direct hit. After a moment the bow of the *New Carissa* slipped below the surface of the sea.

Now all that was left was to attend to the stern. It remained aground at Coos Bay. Much of the fuel had largely been burned off or removed, but what remained could be hazardous. Thus, the next months were devoted to cleaning up the stern section and deciding what to do with it.

Oregon's governor, John Kitzhaber, first requested, then demanded, that the ship's owners remove it from the beach entirely. But the removal became entangled in lawsuits and countersuits about who was ultimately responsible for the grounding and subsequent cleanup. Eventually, the ship's owners paid $25 million for the beach cleanup and restoration. The damage, to this day, continues to be monitored. But the giant, rusting stern still lies in the sands, and now, like the *Peter Iredale*, has become a tourist attraction.

The saga of the *New Carissa* generated extreme interest throughout Oregon, and everyone followed it closely on the evening news and in the papers. The salvage operation was followed like a soap opera, every day bringing some new incredible plot twist in the tale of the ship that would not die. It must have been dismaying to the conscientious people who were working day and night to salvage the ship and protect the shore. But from the outside, it looked very much like a comedy of errors, with the salvage team the butt of a cruel cosmic joke.

The stern of the *New Carissa* still has a story to tell, though. We may be able to send people to the moon or divide an atom;

we can clone sheep and combine the genes of fish with those of strawberries. We can put a plastic heart in a man and a titanium hip in a woman. But we still can't retrieve things from the ocean when they don't want to be retrieved. When it comes to the ocean, we know who is really in charge: not us.

CHAPTER 18

BEWARE THE BERGSCHRUND

Mount Hood Climbing Accident

2002

Cleve Joiner peered over the edge of the crevasse, uncertain of what he might find. Whatever it was, it was likely to be bad. Moments before, he had watched a party of climbers, including his son, slip into the Bergschrund, the great crevasse where Coe Glacier pulls away from Mount Hood. The Bergschrund is a treacherous part of the climb to the top of the mountain. It fluctuates throughout the season and leaves little room for navigation. Sometimes climbers cross the snow bridges that span it; often, though, they choose to go around it. It also marks the beginning of the steepest part of the Mount Hood climb, for just above the Bergschrund climbers must hoist themselves through the chute, lined on both sides by the "Pearly Gates" rocks, that leads them to the summit at 11,239 feet. The Bergschrund is at 10,800 feet.

Attempting to avoid the Bergschrund by going around it is no guarantee of safety, however. The slightest misstep, an instant's inattention, the briefest distraction can send a climber tumbling toward injury or death.

Mount Hood looms above Portland, beckoning climbers.
PHOTO COURTESY PORTLAND DEVELOPMENT COMMISSION

On May 30, 2002, Mount Hood was as crowded as it usually is in the late spring. At 8:30 that morning, climbers were both coming and going, up and down the glacier. A two-man team on its way down included Thomas Hillman, an expert climber, and John Biggs, who had been climbing for about two years. Conditions were slick on that May morning, and Hillman was using the point of his ice ax as an anchor. As the two crept down the glacier roped together, Biggs slipped, sliding about 10 feet. Hillman was just about to self-arrest—anchor himself—when Biggs restored control.

About fifteen minutes behind them was another team, this one of four climbers: Harry Slutter, Chris Kern, Rick Read, and Bill Ward. They were each roped about 35 feet apart from one another. Slutter and Kern had a great deal of experience, Ward somewhat less, and Read was on his first climb.

While these two teams were descending, another group was on its way up. They were mostly paramedics from the Tualatin Valley Fire Department, and they were roped into two teams: Jeff Pierce, fourteen-year-old Cole Joiner, and Jeremiah Moffitt on one team, and Dennis Butler, Selena Maestas, Joiner's father Cleve, and Chad Hashbarger on the other. Pierce's team was waiting above the Bergschrund for Butler's team to make their way around the crevasse.

Without warning Chris Kern found himself sliding down the mountain: The two uppermost climbers, Bill Ward and Rick Read, had apparently slipped. Kern tried to self-arrest, but he was pulled by the other two right down the glacier. Usually, a falling climber will call out so that others below can get out of the way, but this happened so fast that the climbers were tumbling down the mountain without warning.

Slutter, in the meantime, had seen the blur of his falling companions and immediately threw himself into a stable position out of harm's way. But the increasing speed of the other three climbers was setting in motion a chain of events that could not be stopped. They were falling so quickly, and with so much weight, that they pulled Slutter out of his fall arrest position, which under most circumstances could have anchored the entire party. The four climbers were falling headlong toward the Bergschrund. And nine other climbers were in their path.

Hillman, who was busy concentrating on his descent, heard the warning: "Falling!" Looking up, he watched one of the first team careen into his climbing partner Biggs, rolling him down the side of the mountain. Hillman stopped himself, figuring he had 100 feet of rope between him and disaster. But the entangled climbers pulled Hillman down, as he clung to his ax, which was splaying out ice and snow like a miniature plow as he was dragged down the slope.

By this time, the uppermost climber, Ward, had fallen more than 200 feet.

The ascending Tualatin Valley climbers were the next to get caught up in the melee. Pierce heard a shout, raised his eyes, and instantly absorbed the situation. He yelled to his team to get out of the way—"Move right!" he shouted, and then positioned himself against the barrage. Moments later, he too was pulled out of position, and then Cole Joiner and Moffitt were plucked off the mountain in turn, right over the lip of the Bergschrund.

Cleve Joiner watched in horror as his son slid over the edge. The entire incident involving his son had taken about four seconds. The total fall was about 250 feet.

By some miracle one of the ropes remained at the edge of the crevasse. Joiner grabbed in and held on. It was the rope connected to his son, who was on an upper ledge with two other climbers. Clutching the rope with one hand, he fumbled for his cell phone with the other and called for help.

Down in the crevasse, Pierce, who had been knocked unconscious, was waking up. As he awoke, he recalled sliding into the crevasse, where he hit the wall on the downhill side and came to rest on a lower ledge along with three others, in a heap. In all, nine climbers had fallen into the Bergschrund.

The curse of having a large number of climbers on a glacier means that more people can be caught up in a chain-reaction accident such as this one. The blessing is that there are more people to help. The other climbers in the area rushed to the edge of the crevasse. They could see that the nine had fallen about 25 feet. One of the witnesses was Steve Boyer, an emergency room physician from Beaverton, Oregon, and an expert climber. Another was physician Jim Pennington, from Hood River. As the mountain rescue team was being alerted, the climbers at the crevasse lowered Boyer into the Bergschrund to assess the injuries. Boyer and Pierce, who was by now awake, rigged a pulley for hoisting the climbers out of the crevasse and treated those they could.

Mountain rescue arrived, and within an hour or so, all the climbers had been lifted out of the crevasse. Now the trick was to get them off the mountain. Pierce, Cole Joiner, and Slutter were shaken and bruised but essentially all right. The other six were gravely injured. But the rescue was going well—not only were there paramedics among them, but they also had the professional help of Dr. Boyer and Dr. Pennington. Four helicopters from the 1042 Army National Guard unit in Salem hovered overhead as well as two from the 304th Rescue Squadron of the 939th Air Force Reserve Rescue Wing in Portland.

Conditions were good, if a little windy, and everyone was confident that the survivors would be brought home safely. Portland Mountain Rescue and Pacific Northwest Search and Rescue team members made their way up the mountain on foot, joined by teams from American Medical Response's Reach-and-Treat team, the Clackamas County sheriff's office, the U.S. Forest Service, and others. The rescue was also being covered live by more helicopters from the Portland news stations.

Two of the injured climbers had been airlifted to Portland hospitals. The HH-60G Pave Hawk used by the air force was in the process of lifting Jeremiah Moffitt off the mountain. He was lying on a litter.

The Pave Hawk is a sturdy helicopter, but one that can maneuver well under difficult conditions. It weighs about ten tons, and it is designed to survive high-impact landings without catching fire. But mountain conditions are difficult for helicopters. The thinner air and tricky winds around the mountain can make such high-elevation flying work difficult under the best conditions.

Jeff Livick, a rescuer from the ski patrol, was shielding Jeremiah Moffitt from the icy wind whipped up by the helicopter's rotors. Moffitt was conscious and alert. But as he was being lifted out, the wind suddenly kicked up and the pilots lost control of the Pave Hawk. He was in danger of being crushed by a careening helicopter. Then the rescuers—and television viewers—watched in shock as the helicopter swerved toward the side of the mountain, heading in their direction.

Just as the helicopter started to roll, the crew loosed the tether holding Moffitt, and the pilot steered toward the left, narrowly avoiding the rescue teams and thus saving their lives. The pilot could tell he was going to kill everyone in his path unless he could maneuver the helicopter out of the way. Livick saw the rotor splinter as it smashed into the side of the mountain. The helicopter crashed, then rolled seven times, coming to rest 1,000 feet below. The crew was thrown out of the cockpit and onto the slopes. The flight engineer was still attached by his gunbelt webbing, and the helicopter rolled over him twice before the weight of the falling helicopter tore the webbing away. Footage of the dramatic crash was replayed on television across the world.

Miraculously, none of the flight crew—or the people on the ground—died as a result. By evening all the rest of the injured climbers and crew had been brought down the mountain or flown out on backup helicopters. But three climbers would die of their massive crush injuries: Read, Ward, and Biggs. And having to rescue the rescuers—the three members of the flight crew—made the operation that much more perilous.

CHAPTER 19

WHEN LIGHTNING STRIKES

The Biscuit Fire

2002

The Biscuit Fire, named for the hill where it first sparked, arrived on July 13, 2002, brought courtesy of 12,000 lightning strikes on dry summer grass and brush across remote areas of southwest Oregon and northern California. Hundreds of fires were ignited, and four of them—the Florence and West Florence and the Biscuit and Sour Biscuit—converged in late July.

Most of the area that was burned was in the Siskiyou and Six Rivers National Forests, eventually reaching 499,965 acres. It burned through the Kalmiopsis Wilderness; it raged through much of the Illinois River Valley, almost to the Rogue River in the north, stopping just 10 miles east of Brookings, Oregon, on the coast. Four houses and ten other buildings were lost, as well as a Boy Scout camp and other recreational buildings. No one died.

What is remarkable about the Biscuit Fire, however, is effort that went into suppressing it. More than 7,000 firefighters were dispatched to fight it, with a battalion of water tankers, fire engines, airplanes, and helicopters. More was spent fighting the Biscuit Fire than had ever been spent on any other wildfire: $155 million. Yet all the work and money had little effect on the fire. Was it worth it?

Jerry and Gayle Sorenson have some insight. Sorenson is a logger, fishing guide, and writer who lives at Oak Flat, a tiny community along the Illinois River. Oak Flat is deep within the Siskyou National Forest, and the Sorensons are the only permanent residents. Their nine neighbors are seasonal, and the Sorensons keep an eye out on their properties. Oak Flat is so small and remote that it doesn't even have postal service. But it is very beautiful in the unique way of the Siskyou Forest and Kalmiopsis—rocky crags, ancient meadows, forests of pine, fir, and cedar.

Above the pines fire lookouts keep a watchful eye on the Siskyou throughout the summer. In 2003 they were especially vigilant in the early part of July, the height of fire season. On July 12, they observed a number of lightning strikes. No one was worried—such strikes are normal during the summer—but the Forest Service flew some reconnaissance missions over the Kalmiopsis Wilderness to monitor them. Small fires were observed by July 16, including a fifty-acre fire near Oak Flat. The Forest Service decided to let it burn, given that it was remote and likely impossible to contain. Besides, there didn't seem to be any smoke jumpers available when they asked the local office. Smoke jumpers might have been able to contain the fire at this stage. But they were in Colorado, cleaning up after another fire, and the Siskiyou Forest was not a big priority.

Letting fire burn is controversial. It seems to go against what we've all been taught about forest fires. For decades Smokey the Bear has taught schoolchildren that only they can prevent forest fires, leaving the impression that people cause most of them. Yet people cause only about 40 percent of forest fires. Most fires, like the Biscuit Fire, are ignited by lightning.

Regardless of how they start, the urge to suppress them is understandable. After fires such as the Tillamook Burn, which destroyed the economy of the towns that relied on the Tillamook forest, the U.S. Forest Service began to professionalize their firefighters. They sought to find a way to fight fires in a more systematic and scientific way. Yet it turns out that our fire-suppressing tendencies may have left us more vulnerable to fire, not less.

That's because fire has always been part of the ecosystem of the West. It's likely that there have always been catastrophic fires, just as there have always been catastrophic windstorms. But until the West was settled by ranchers, loggers, and farmers, fire was a regular summer event. It didn't go very far or burn very much—evidence from giant trees harvested in the 1800s shows that the fires stayed at the level of the grass and brush, burning them off but not harming the trees. Indeed, it appears that the forests were actually less brushy than they are now. This low level of fuel would produce a steady fire, but one that would not crown and spread wildly through the land. The more fires we put out, the more dangerous fuels build up. Thus when fires do happen—as is inevitable—they are more severe.

Some forests are managed with controlled burns to mimic these conditions. But most are not, and such burns were not apparently part of the practice of forest management in the Siskiyou. By nightfall on July 16, the small 50-acre fire had grown to 600 acres. It had crowned and was about to explode out of its wilderness boundaries. Two days later, it was a 1,600-acre fire.

Self-reliance is characteristic of those who live in wild lands, a prudent strategy since in an emergency there may not be anyone else around to help. Jerry and Gayle Sorenson have embraced this philosophy and carefully ready themselves for fire each summer. They dig a wide dirt border around their property, careful to dig it down to the mineral soil so that nothing inflammable remains. The roof of their house is metal, they clear brush and small trees away from the house, and they make sure to water regularly. They know that fire is part of the normal passing of the season, and they know that it is their responsibility to work with it and give it its due.

So they alertly waited as the fire advanced. By July 19, it was speeding up. The Oregon Department of Forestry paid a call on the Sorensons to check out Oak Flat and see what was there. They were mapping out the area to see what buildings should be protected. Over the next few days, the Sorensons and various firefighting officials reconnoitered. The Sorensons began alerting their neighbors that their houses might be in danger, while firefighters dug fire trails and cleared brush from around the neighboring houses. Neighbors began arriving to prepare for fire, just in case. One put in a sprinkler system around his house, as well as the building that protected his generator. On July 21, the Biscuit and Sour Biscuit fires converged. Now there were two large fires, the Florence fire, near the Sorensons, and the Biscuit fire.

On July 23, the Forest Service made plans to do some aerial backburning. One way to stop a fire is to set smaller fires that can be controlled. This way, the large fire that is advancing will be deprived of fuel. The Forest Service targeted 1,000 acres from Flat Top Mountain, near the Sorenson homestead, to Oak Flat, planning to burn them. They were also digging a fire line to contain this backburn.

The Biscuit Fire covered 499,965 acres. It cost $155 million—but there were no fatalities. U.S. FOREST SERVICE

By July 24, Sorenson was concerned. He could see fires in the nearby hills, and he began strengthening his fire trail. The Sorensons now figured the fire was inevitable, and sure enough about 4 P.M., the fire on York Butte, a nearby hill, exploded. It would soon reach Oak Flat. The firefighters told the Sorensons and their neighbors to leave and gave them fifteen minutes to evacuate.

Jerry and Gayle Sorenson decided to remain. They knew their property was fire-safe, and they had been watering the grass around the house so it would not ignite. But they didn't account for Forest Service plans, and to their surprise, firefighters set backburns behind the house of one of their neighbors and in the Sorensons' pasture. They gave the couple two aluminum fire shelters—last-resort emergency shelters that wildfire fighters hope will save them when they are about to be engulfed by a ranging forest fire—and then left.

The next day, before dawn, the fire arrived at Oak Flat. It burned out part of the Sorensons' water line, cutting off their water supply, and it burned some of their neighbors' outbuildings. The houses themselves were safe. They called the neighbors. Oak Flat had survived.

Or so Jerry Sorenson thought. The day dawned hotter than ever, and the Forest Service fire behavior analyst foresaw the day bringing "advanced extreme" fire behavior. The firefighters were back at Oak Flat the next morning, cutting brush along the Illinois River and digging a new fire line along the ridge above Oak Flat. And in the afternoon, they set more backburns—but these charred what was left of the Sorensons' water line, the part nearest the creek. And it didn't do any good, because by the following afternoon, the fire line that was meant to contain the backfire had been breached.

Sorensen went to inspect the fire about 6 A.M. on July 27. It was meandering back down the ridge. Sorenson writes that "had firefighters jumped on the backfire early that morning or the previous night, I believe it could have been controlled." As it was, however, all he could do was to bulldoze another fire line and hope for the best. He spent the early afternoon reinstalling the water line so he could water down his property if necessary.

But about an hour after he finished, in the hottest part of the day, the backburn completely overtook the fire line and sped toward Oak Flat. The firefighters withdrew to the relative safety of the Sorenson property—the fire was heading straight for them. It destroyed three of the houses in Oak Flat. It incinerated Sorenson's own timber, as well as the brand-new water line. The helicopter that was brought in to pour water on the fire ended up blowing up some of the houses' propane tanks.

After the fire roared through Oak Flat, it moved south along the Illinois River for 14 miles, burning up the McCaleb Ranch Boy Scout Camp, privately held forest, and national forest with frightening speed.

Though the major portion of the fire had now passed them by, the Sorensons still had a lot of work to do. They had to keep an eye out for "hot spots" of smoldering debris that could suddenly flare up if they got enough oxygen. On July 29, they finished restoring the water line, which was lucky: They saw a large flare-up of the fire that they were able to extinguish with their replumbed water.

Their work was finally over by August 3. But the Biscuit Fire raged on for a month after that and did its worst damage throughout August. Toward the end of July, firefighters planned fire lines that would systematically contain the major zones of the fire, plans that included both digging new breaks and putting to use existing roads. The goal was to set backburns within these zones—ironically, however, the planned backburn was 34,000 acres, larger than the fires being fought already. They alerted residents in the area that the backburns might be alarming and very smoky; indeed, they predicted that far more smoke would come from the fires that they set than from existing fires. For residents in the Siskiyou, the constant presence of smoke was both annoying and worrisome, and the decision to begin these backburns in the hottest, driest month of the year raised local eyebrows.

By August 4, the fire had reached 240,000 acres, and by the 21st, the unbearably smoky blazes—both the original fire and all the fires that were intended to stop it—had consumed 740 square miles.

We may have painted ourselves into a corner when it comes to fighting fires—what writer Edward Tenner calls the revenge of unintended consequences. By suppressing all the fires, the fire danger becomes much worse. But the natural remedy, which would be allowing them to burn, invites catastrophe. Especially considering we've let the fuel build up in the forest for nearly a century. Setting backburns can be a useful approach, since it does what natural wildfires are supposed to do, but in drought conditions, the backburn may backfire, as happened in the Biscuit Fire.

There is a great deal of debate about how to solve this dilemma. Jerry Sorenson thinks that a sensible plan would encompass a variety of tactics, from judicious burning during the spring and fall when it's not as dry to targeted and early use of smoke jumpers; the plan would use the wisdom of local residents in combination with the expertise of the U.S. Forest Service—not in opposition to it—especially since firefighters are almost always from outside local areas. It would encourage homeowners to be responsible for keeping their property firesafe. Most of all, it would think things through better so that decisions are made with greater thought to their consequences.

The Biscuit Fire cleanup and salvage brought new controversy—controversy that is ongoing, controversy that surrounds salvage. Some foresters believe that logging the salvageable trees is good for the forest and the local economy. It's certainly good for some parts of the economy, but whether it's good for the forest is another matter. Other foresters point out that salvage logging leaves a great deal of slash and other inflammable materials behind, paradoxically increasing the danger of fire. The Tillamook Burn was heavily logged for salvage, and three major fires erupted in the area of the burn after this practice began.

A forest recovers from fires amazingly fast, even using a human scale of time. Even though the Biscuit Fire burned more than 740 square miles, it was not as catastrophic as first feared. It burned in what is known as a mosaic pattern—bits of unscathed land, other bits of low-intensity burn, and bits of severe burn. More than 60 percent of the area encompassed by the burn was comparatively unharmed, burning a little or not at all. Just 16 percent of the area was burned severely. The Kalmiopsis Wilderness is already recovering, and people are hiking there once more.

The end of summer announces itself suddenly in Oregon. One evening, you notice a chill in the air and you have to put on a sweater. That's when you know it's the end of fire season. The fire was officially contained—at least the Oregon part of it—on August 22, but it didn't really die out until the weather shifted in late August and early September. By September 5, moist air and lower temperatures finally allowed the fire to be suppressed. That's pretty much how a major fire is contained: with a lot of help from the weather. Ultimately, the Biscuit Fire stopped itself, at a cost of $155 million to let it do so.

CHAPTER 20

FATAL ERROR

The Sinking of the *Taki-Tooo*

2003

On a late spring day in 2003, crossing the bar from Tillamook Bay to the Pacific Ocean, nineteen people were swept from a 32-foot charter fishing boat, the *Taki-Tooo*. Eleven people died, eight were injured, and it was one of the worst U.S. marine accidents in years. Coast Guard officers had seen the whole thing happen and had arrived in five minutes, but by then it was too late for most of the victims. Everyone, from the federal authorities to the families involved to casual observers, wanted to know what went wrong.

The *Taki-Tooo*'s home port was Garibaldi, Oregon, a coastal village on Tillamook Bay along the Pacific Ocean. Early in the morning on June 14—the Saturday before Father's Day—seventeen men and two women stood about the marina at the dock of Garibaldi Charters, bantering with one another as they donned their slickers and rubber boots. They were looking forward to a day of fishing. Just a few miles west of Garibaldi were beautiful reefs that lured rockfish and black sea bass, sea trout and ling cod, yelloweye and salmon, reefs that also lured scores of fisherman.

While the *Taki-Tooo*'s passengers joked, the skipper, Doug Davis, was chatting with his twenty-two-year-old deckhand, Tamara Buell, daughter of the owners of Garibaldi Charters. Davis had been monitoring the weather and the conditions of the sea. He was a cheerful person and, according to the National Transportation Safety Board (NTSB) report, "had bounced in the door that morning . . . he was joking with people and laughing." But he and Tamara Buell looked at the surf conditions and privately decided they were too volatile to put out their crab pots, since in choppy seas their lines can entangle boat engines. The smaller boats had already decided not to go out at all—in fact the Coast Guard wouldn't let them—and the *Taki-Tooo* had taken on some of their passengers.

The surf was high that morning, long, high swells of 8 to 12 feet. Far to the north, off the coasts of Canada and Alaska, strong storms had churned up the Pacific and sent swells toward Oregon, where they were pushed even higher by the prevailing westerly winds. At about 3:30 that morning, the Coast Guard closed the bar at Tillamook Bay to small craft, as well as to charter boats that were not approved for high surf. It was not the wind and the waves alone creating these dangerous conditions. The bar just west of Tillamook Bay is a notorious trap for ships. And the action of the tide didn't help either, for an ebbing tide creates much havoc for boats when the water pulled by the tide collides with the swells moving toward shore.

But the well-maintained *Taki-Tooo* was approved for such surf conditions. Doug Davis was sixty-six years old and had operated charter fishing vessels for more than twenty-six years. He was both beloved and trusted. He had crossed the Tillamook bar more than a thousand times.

Davis and his wife owned Davis Fisheries, Inc., and the *Taki-Tooo* was one of its assets. They had owned Garibaldi Charters as well but sold the business. The new owners, Mick Buell and his wife, leased the *Taki-Tooo* from Davis, whom they had known many years. They were also happy to hire Davis to operate it, since he was much sought-after by previous customers. Over the years, first under Davis's stewardship and then under the Buells', Garibaldi Charters had developed a good reputation, for the quality of both its skippers and its craft.

Just before 6 A.M., Davis and Tamara Buell brought their seventeen passengers aboard. Davis gave a little safety talk, and he told his passengers that if they wanted to put on a life jacket, it was up to them, and that the jackets could be found in the cabin, stored in marked bins underneath the table. He told them to "just ask us if you need help getting them on or anything," though he didn't show them how to use the life jackets. Then Davis told them that the vessel had on board a first-aid kit and emergency equipment such as flares, a life raft, and a throw ring. And he described his own safety rules: no alcohol, no drugs, no dumping trash over the side. He said that they wouldn't put out the crab pots, since the seas were rough.

Among the passengers were experienced fishermen, including Mark Hamlett from Portland, and one who had never before fished on saltwater, Ed Loll, from Cedar Rapids, Iowa. He was visiting his son Brian Loll—the son-in-law of Mark Hamlett—for Father's Day. He had been anticipating this trip with great excitement and announced that no matter what else happened, he would be catching a bigger fish than his son.

Four boats set out at 6 A.M.: the *Norwester,* the *Oakland Pilot,* the *D&D,* and the *Taki-Tooo*. Most passengers stood about the deck of the *Taki-Tooo* in their rain gear, taking in the sights along scenic Tillamook Bay. By 6:45 the *Taki-Tooo* had reached the north jetty leading to the bay. It circled the water, looking for a lull in the surf that would allow a safe crossing. The tide was ebbing and the swells were large, and the four charter boats hovered near the Tillamook Bay jetties, waiting for conditions to improve.

The Tillamook bar is tricky. Any bar is tricky, since the waters are shallow and the sands beneath them shift, rising and falling. The Tillamook bar is narrow and difficult to maneuver, especially during an ebbing tide, when the force of the water going out clashes with the force of heavy seas coming in. The Tillamook bar is about a mile square, a mile square of choppy and unforgiving waters, even on good days.

At 6:50 the *Norwester* saw an opening and headed for the open ocean. But the skipper radioed the *Taki-Tooo* and advised them to wait—it "wasn't worth it," and there were a lot of floating logs at the tips of the jetties, logs that he narrowly avoided. Over on the *Oakland Pilot,* the skipper told his passengers to sit down for the crossing, and as he took his boat over, he too had to dodge the logs. The *D&D* started over the bar next, at about 7:00. The pilot seemed to have little trouble, but his passengers were unnerved, and a number of them put on their life jackets and left them on for the day. One passenger said he never again would cross the bar without a life jacket.

Then it was the *Taki-Tooo*'s turn. While the other boats were crossing, the *Taki-Tooo* was hovering, assessing conditions. Twelve people were on the open deck, including Davis and Buell on the flying bridge. Something prompted Davis to cross. But just as he did, the boat rode up and over a large swell, and then the waves got even larger. Tamara Buell heard Davis say, "I didn't want to get into this." Then he threw the engines into reverse or astern power—it is not clear which—to stabilize the vessel in the wave.

Following all of this were the Coast Guard tower watch at the end of the north jetty and Mick Buell, who had driven to the jetty to watch his boats, the *Taki-Tooo* and the *D&D*, cross the bar. Both observed the *Taki-Tooo* depart and followed its progress. The Coast Guard watch saw the boat pass frighteningly close to the tip of the north jetty. The *Taki-Tooo* swerved northward just as a large swell approached from the west—then it fell into a trough between the waves. And the next thing that happened was a 15-foot wave hit the *Taki-Tooo* and capsized it.

As Tamara Buell later told NTSB investigators:

> When we were going over the first wave, it kind of got us tilted, when [Davis] backed up, I saw the wave coming and I told everybody to hold on, I didn't look back to see where everybody was. I said, "Hold on." And I grabbed onto the boat and we went over it and . . . I was telling somebody that that was probably about a 9- or 10-foot wave. But, right on the other side of it . . . I saw a huge one building, and it was really steep and it was coming straight at us. And somehow, I am not really clear on . . . whether it was the captain that had turned to [the] boat or whether we were still turning from sliding down the back of the wave, but somehow we got completely sideways to it. And my first impression was that he was trying to turn the boat around to ride with it. But, we got completely sideways to the wave and by the time it was real close, I could tell that we were going to go over. And it was probably about 12 to 15 feet because I was looking up at it. And it just smashed in the side of the boat and went over.

The next thing anyone knew, thirteen people were in the water, then most of them disappeared. Mick Buell saw that five people had managed to grab the life raft and climb aboard, but seconds later, it too capsized and they simply vanished in the cold water. Tamara managed to wriggle out of her boots, pants, and jacket, and began swimming to shore. One of the passengers, a twenty-eight-year-old man, tried to reach the life raft half a dozen times but could not hold onto it. However, he was washed to shore in the waves and made it out alive, to the relief of horrified bystanders.

Not everyone was in the water. One person was somehow washed from the open deck into the cabin. Five others were already there. One of them was Mark Hamlett, a seasoned fisherman who had once fished commercially out of Brookings, Oregon. He had been standing next to the flying bridge, chatting with Davis and watching the other three boats cross the bar. He could tell Davis was concentrating, and he too was concerned—seas were rough, and the *Taki-Tooo* was small enough to be vulnerable to swells that size. Hamlett saw the large swell approaching and hurried to the deck below, afraid that the wave would break over the *Taki-Tooo*. When the wave hit the boat and capsized it, the boat rolled one-and-a-half times, sending gear hurtling through the air and the people below smashing into the walls and ceiling of the cabin.

No one was wearing a life vest.

Mark's son Chris was sitting in the cabin, drinking coffee on the port side, watching out the window. He noticed with alarm the giant wave headed in their direction. When the wave hit, he said, it was like being in a washing machine. He couldn't get air. He heard his brother-in-law, Brian Loll, scream, "Oh my God!"

The cabin was awash in seawater. The boat came to rest upside down, displaying a peculiar green light from the windows, which were now underwater. Thinking fast, Mark Hamlett groped around as best he could, given that he and the others were upside down, and found the cabinet with the life jackets. He passed them out to those inside. Hamlett, his two sons, his son-in-law Brian Loll, and Brian's father Ed put on their life jackets. The air pocket in the boat bought them all some time. But no one knew how they were going to get out, since the hatch and windows were below the water level.

Then the boat rolled again and a window broke. Water began to pour into the cabin. It was time to get out. One person made it out of the cabin door. The others chose the windows. But now they had to take off their life jackets to get through. Chris Hamlett took off his life jacket, swam out, then put his life jacket back on over his head and floated toward shore, where folks had begun to gather. They helped him out of the water. Other passengers did similar things—taking off their life jackets to get through the window and then tying them on to their arms or clinging to them desperately. Mark Hamlett and Brian Loll begged Ed Loll to leave, but he seemed overwhelmed and could not. Brian kept asking, "Dad, are you all right?" At first, he appeared to be—he said he was fine. But according to the passengers in the cabin, he sat down, moaned a little, and fell silent.

Ed had always been a large, decisive man, but he had had two heart attacks and a hip replaced. And the water was cold—fifty-two degrees. Most people who die in the water do so in the first few minutes, from the shock of the cold and subsequent failure to breathe or sustain the heart, rather than slowly freezing to death. When a person who is not mentally prepared for the cold of the water is thrown into temperatures that low, the shock of the cold alone can be fatal—the surprise of the cold water induces a large gasp, then rapid breathing, a faster heartbeat, and increased blood pressure. The strain on the heart often kills older, less healthy persons, but it can be deadly to anyone who is not expecting it. If they manage to survive the first two or three minutes, they will have to contend with immersion in cold water, which can have the opposite effect on the heart: It slows down, eventually stopping altogether. Of the nine bodies recovered, all were observed to have had cardiac arrest and hypothermia.

Heartsick at his father's inaction, Brian Loll nonetheless had his own survival to consider, and finally he decided that it was now or never. He took off his life jacket to squeeze through the cabin window. Unlike the others, Brian lost hold of his life jacket. Still, somehow he managed to swim to a place about 200 feet offshore, waded the rest of the way, and then collapsed on the beach.

The Coast Guard watch at the north jetty had alerted the Coast Guard station at Tillamook Bay at 7:16, as soon as he saw that the *Taki-Tooo* had capsized, and two minutes after the call, the search-and-rescue helicopters, based 30 miles north in Astoria, were requested. Two boats sped out to the scene of the accident, and area hospitals, fire stations, and paramedics were on full alert. Yet it was too late for them to do anything except retrieve as many bodies as they could. One of those retrieved was Ed Loll, who was still in the cabin of the *Taki-Tooo* when it washed ashore less than half an hour later.

About 200 people have lost their lives along the Tillamook bar since records for such things have been kept. It's been the site of some spectacular shipwrecks, including the *Argo*, the

Detroit, the *Ida Schnauer,* the *Millie Bond,* the *Phoenix,* the *Tyee,* and the *Vida.* Though none were as deadly, several of these wrecks were similar to that of the *Taki-Tooo*—the ships got caught in a trough while crossing the bar and then capsized. Indeed, the jetties were built precisely to minimize accidents over the bar, but the NTSB, in their report on the *Taki-Tooo,* noted that the condition of the jetties—due to wear and tear—had been objectively deteriorating. That is, they were not only thought to be in bad shape by the seagoing vessels that used them to cross the bar, but also according to the length that the Army Corps of Engineers, who built and maintain them, says they should be. The corps found that storms have been getting worse in the Pacific in recent years, resulting in stronger and more dangerous waves. Still, the NTSB found that the channel was deep enough and the bar itself was not the main cause of the accident.

The decision to cross the bar, however, was another story. While technically not forbidden to cross it—the *Taki-Tooo* was in good standing and had been inspected—the option to stay home was there. Several other charter operators had elected to do just that on June 14, even though they were cleared to leave the harbor. Davis himself had turned back in the past, perhaps fifty or sixty times, according to one of his friends and fellow skippers, Jim Weisberg. But there was no formal policy at Garibaldi Charters. It was left to the discretion of the skipper. And there was a lot of subtle pressure to go out. Davis had been especially requested for this trip. It was Father's Day weekend. Even Mark Hamlett felt that pressure: At one point he had had a twinge of doubt about whether they should go. But Ed really wanted to—he really wanted to catch a big fish on the beautiful Pacific Ocean.

And the decision not to have the passengers wear life jackets was another issue that the NTSB raised. Why hadn't Davis insisted that his passengers wear them? Of the eight people who survived the capsizing of the *Taki-Tooo,* six wore life jackets. Of the eleven who died, only one wore his. No one put on a life jacket until the boat capsized.

Still, it's not that simple. There is no Coast Guard rule that says you must wear a life jacket, even though they're recommended. A little-known rule requires passengers to wear them *when possible,* but no citations have ever been written on Tillamook Bay to enforce this rule, so it was not taken very seriously—if anyone even knew about it. After the accident there was much discussion about the failure to wear life jackets or even to explain carefully where they were and how to put them on, with many indignant over the absence of such a simple safety precaution.

That the most seasoned fisherman and the novices alike failed to wear them makes the case more complex. Davis and Buell offered to assist anyone who wanted a life jacket, but no one took them up on this offer, and they could not, of course, force adults to wear them. Perhaps, like many of us, their passengers were inured to safety lectures, having learned to ignore them on airplane flights. Or perhaps they were just following habit. Lots of people, maybe most people, don't wear life jackets. They may put them on their children, but they think to themselves—if they think about it at all—that the bulky, uncomfortable jackets are too inconvenient, that they themselves are good swimmers and can take a dip in the ocean, or simply that nothing will happen. Life jackets are a reminder that something terrible might happen.

And that's precisely why charter boat operators don't require them: It is uncomfortable for the passengers. As Tron Buell, master of the *D&D* and brother of Tamara Buell observed to the NTSB, if passengers were required to wear life jackets by the Coast Guard when they crossed the bar, they would comply without thought.

"But for us to tell them they have to do it, it just scares the hell out of them."

Bibliography

DEATH AND DESTRUCTION IN ITS WAKE: The Heppner Flood (1903)

DenOuden, Bob. "Without a Second's Warning: The Heppner Flood of 1903," *Oregon Historical Quarterly*, Vol. 105, 2004, pp. 108–19.

Heppner Gazette. June 18, 1903, p. 1.

Heppner Gazette Times. June 11, 1953.

Matlock, Leslie L., and O. M. Yeager. *A Wild Night Ride: Two Men's Heroic Race against the Heppner Flood of 1903*. Wallowa, Ore.: Bear Creek Press, 2002.

DEAD MAN'S HOTEL: The Wreck of the *Mimi* (1913)

Gibbs, James. *Shipwrecks of the Pacific Coast*. Portland: Binford & Mort, 1957.

Grover, David. *The Unforgiving Coast: Maritime Disasters of the Pacific Northwest*. Corvallis: Oregon State University Press, 2002.

Marshall, Don. *Oregon Shipwrecks*. Portland: Binford & Mort, 1984.

PORT TOWN IN FLAMES: The Astoria Fire (1922)

Friedman, Ralph. *A Touch of Oregon: Lovesong to a State*. New York: Ballantine, 1970.

Morning Oregonian. September 9, 1922.

———. September 10, 1922.

Penttila, Bryan. *Columbia River: The Astoria Odyssey*. Portland: Frank Amato Publications, 2003.

DANGEROUS SLOPES:
The Mazamas on Coe Glacier (1927)

The Cloud Cap Inn, Coopers Spur, Oregon, Web site: www.mounthoodhistory.com/Buildings/cloudcapinn.html.

MacNeil, Fred H. *Wy'east: The Mountain. A Chronicle of Mt. Hood.* Portland: The Metropolitan Press, 1937.

Oregonian. July 18, 1927.

"JUST ONE MORE LOG":
The Tillamook Burn (1933)

Friedman, Ralph. *In Search of Western Oregon.* Caldwell, Idaho: Caxton, 1990.

Kemp, J. Larry. *Epitaph for the Giants: The Story of the Tillamook Burn.* Portland: Touchstone Press, 1967.

Laskin, David. *Rains All the Time: A Connoisseur's History of Weather in the Pacific Northwest.* Seattle: Sasquatch, 1997.

Tenner, Edward. *Why Things Bite Back: Technology and the Revenge of the Unintended Consequences.* New York: Vintage, 1996.

Wells, Gail. *The Tillamook: A Created Forest Comes of Age.* Corvallis: Oregon State University Press, 1999.

HERE TODAY, GONE TOMORROW:
The Vanport Flood (1948)

Maben, Manly. *Vanport.* Portland: Oregon Historical Society Press, 1987.

McElderry, Stuart. "Vanport Conspiracy Rumors and Social Relations in Portland, 1940–1950," *Oregon Historical Quarterly,* Vol. 99, 1998, pp. 134–63.

Oregonian. May 31, 1948.

———. June 1, 1948.

ARCTIC ILLUSIONS: Three Blizzards (1950)

Laskin, David. *Rains All the Time: A Connoisseur's History of Weather in the Pacific Northwest.* Seattle: Sasquatch, 1997.

"Local Notable Historical Storms and Data: Some of the Area's Snowstorms," NOAA Web site: www.wrh.noaa.gov/pqr/past storms/snow.php.

Oregonian. January 5, 1950.

———. January 9, 1950.

———. January 11, 1950.

———. January 14, 1950.

———. January 15, 1950.

———. January 19, 1950.

———. January 21, 1950.

The Oregon Statesman. January 14, 1950.

———. January 18, 1950.

———. January 20, 1950.

———. January 25, 1950.

———. January 26, 1950.

AN OCTOBER ODDITY: The Columbus Day Storm (1962)

Laskin, David. *Rains All the Time: A Connoisseur's History of Weather in the Pacific Northwest.* Seattle: Sasquatch, 1997.

Oregonian. "Reporter recounts ordeal of ride in teeth of hurricane," October 13, 1962, p. 39.

———. October 14, 1962.

A COASTAL CATASTROPHE:
Tsunami (1964)

Drye, Willie. "California Tsunami Victims Recall 1964's Killer Waves," *National Geographic News,* January 21, 2005, National Geographic Web site: http://news.nationalgeographic.com/news/2005/01/0121_050121_1964_tsunami.html.

"The Great Alaskan Earthquake and Tsunamis of 1964," NOAA Web site: http://wcatwc.arh.noaa.gov/64quake.htm.

Oregonian. March 29, 1964.

A WET CHRISTMAS:
The Willamette River Flood (1964)

Miller, George R. "The Great Willamette River Flood of 1861," *Oregon Historical Quarterly,* Vol. 100, 1999, pp. 182–207.

Oregonian. "Flood Eats into Town," December 25, 1964.

———. December 26, 1964.

———. December 27, 1964.

MAYDAY IN AUGUST:
The Brookings-Harbor Rescues (1972)

Gibney, Jayne. *There Were No Birds: A Memoir of the Storm of '72, Brookings, Oregon.* Brookings: Every Word Counts, 2000.

U.S. Coast Guard. "Loss of Numerous Vessels during Heavy Weather in the Vicinity of Chetco River, Oregon on or about 16 August 1972; with Loss of Life," *Marine Casualty Report* (USCG/NTSB Mar 74-7), Washington, D.C.: USCG, 1974.

"WE'RE GOING DOWN":
The Last Journey of Flight 173 (1978)

National Transportation Safety Board. *Aircraft Incident Report* (NTSB-AAR-79-7), Washington, D.C.: NTSB, 1979.
Oregonian. December 28, 1978.
———. December 29, 1978.
———. December 30, 1978.

"THIS IS IT!":
The Eruption of Mount St. Helens (1980)

"Cascade Volcano Observatory. Mount St. Helens, Washington—May 18, 1980 Eruption," United States Geological Service Web site: http://Vulcan.wr.usgs.gov/Volcanoes/MSH/May18/framework.html.
Oregonian. May 19, 1980.
———. May 23, 1980.
———. May 24, 1980.
———. June 13, 1980.
Parchman, Frank. *Echoes of Fury: The 1980 Eruption of Mt. St. Helens and the Lives It Changed Forever.* Kenmore, Wash.: Epicenter Press, 2005.
Tilling, R. I., L. Topinka, and D. A. Swanson. *Eruptions of Mount St. Helens: Past, Present, and Future* (USGS Special Interest Publication), Washington, D.C.: United States Geological Service, 1990.

TRAGEDY ON MOUNT HOOD:
The Oregon Episcopal School Climb (1986)

Oregonian. May 15, 1986.
———. May 16, 1986.

Seattle Times. May 22, 1986.

———. June 25, 1986.

———. July 17, 1986.

———. July 18, 1986.

BURNING FIELDS:

Chain-Reaction Car Accident (1988)

Emergency Management Plan. *Dust Storms*. Salem: State of Oregon, 2004.

Eugene Register-Guard. August 5, 1988.

Oregonian. August 5, 1988.

Salem Statesman-Journal. August 5, 1988.

Tri-City Herald. September 26, 1999.

A WET AND WILD WINTER:

Raging Waters (1995–1996)

KATU. "Wild winter" (videorecording). Seattle: Fisher Broadcasting, 1996.

Oregonian. February 8, 1996.

———. February 9, 1996.

———. February 10, 1996.

Taylor, George H. "The Great Flood of 1996," Oregon Climatology Service Web site: http://www.ocs.orst.edu/reports/flood96/Flood2.html.

COOS BAY CATASTROPHE:

The Wreck of the *New Carissa* (1999)

Hall, M. J. *Crisis on the Coast: Federal On-Scene Coordinator's Report and Assessment of M/V NEW CARISSA Oil Spill Response* (Vols. 1 and 2), Portland: U.S. Coast Guard Marine Safety Office, 1999.

"Key Information on the *New Carissa* Oil Spill Final Restoration Plan." Oregon Fish and Wildlife Office, U.S. Fish and Wildlife Web site: www.fws.gov/oregonfwo/InfED/TopicsOfInterest .html.

Pacific States and British Columbia Oil Spill Task Force. 2003.

BEWARE THE BERGSCHRUND:

Mount Hood Climbing Accident (2002)

"Copter Crashes during Mount Hood Rescue," CNN Web site: http://archives.cnn.com/2002/US/05/03/oregon.mthood .accident/.

Gonzales, L. "The Slipping Point: Disaster on Mount Hood," *National Geographic Adventure,* September 2002.

Press release, May 31, 2002, Portland Mountain Rescue Web site: www.pmru.org.

WHEN LIGHTNING STRIKES:

The Biscuit Fire (2002)

Gantenbein, Douglas. "We're Toast," *Outside,* June 2003, *Outside* magazine Web site: outside.away.com/outside/features/ 200306/200306_were_toast_1.html.

Sheley, Chuck. "A Final Look at the Biscuit Fire—Is the Initial Attack System Broken?" National Smokejumper Association Web site: www.smokejumpers.com/opinion/item.php?opinion_ id=263.

Sorenson, Jerry. "Who Needs Help Like This?" *Forest,* Fall 2003, *Forest* magazine Web site: www.fseee.org/index.html?page= http%3A//www.fseee.org/forestmag/0303sorensen.shtml.

Sullivan, William L. "The View from Ground Zero at Oregon's Biggest Fire in 100 Years," *High Country News,* December 2002.

Tenner, Edward. *Why Things Bite Back: Technology and the Revenge of Unintended Consequences.* New York: Vintage, 1996.

Wilderness Society. "Summary of the Biscuit Complex Fire, Oregon/California. July 13–September 5, 2002," Wilderness Society Web site: http://www.wilderness.org/Library/Documents/Wildfire Summary_Biscuit.cfm.

FATAL ERROR:

The Sinking of the *Taki-Tooo* (2003)

Donahue, Bill. "The Tragedy of Tillamook Bay," *Field and Stream* Web site: http://www.fieldandstream.com/fieldstream/fishing/saltwater/article/0,13199,572251,00.html.

National Transportation Safety Board. *Capsizing of US Small Passenger Vessel* Taki-Tooo, *Tillamook Bay Inlet, Oregon* (Marine Accident Report NTSB/MAR-05/02. PB2005-916402. Notation 7582B), Washington, D.C.: NTSB, 2005.

Oregonian. "Taki-Tooo Capsizing Is Blamed on Skipper," June 29, 2005.

About the Author

RACHEL DRESBECK is a writer and editor who lives in Portland, Oregon, with her husband, two children, and dog. Her previous Globe Pequot books include *Insiders' Guide to Portland, Oregon*. The daughter of two historians, she has long meditated on the scope and variety of disasters and how they shape human experience and test our will.